**UNLEARN HABITS THAT KEEP YOU CHAINED
AND IGNITE A LIFE OF LASTING CHANGE.**

Capt. Surajmani Tuluri

BLUEROSE PUBLISHERS
India | U.K.

Copyright © Surajmani Tuluri 2024

All rights reserved by author. No part of this publication may be reproduced, stored in a retrieval system or transmitted in any form or by any means, electronic, mechanical, photocopying, recording or otherwise, without the prior permission of the author. Although every precaution has been taken to verify the accuracy of the information contained herein, the publisher assume no responsibility for any errors or omissions. No liability is assumed for damages that may result from the use of information contained within.

BlueRose Publishers takes no responsibility for any damages, losses, or liabilities that may arise from the use or misuse of the information, products, or services provided in this publication.

For permissions requests or inquiries regarding this publication, please contact:

BLUEROSE PUBLISHERS
www.BlueRoseONE.com
info@bluerosepublishers.com
+91 8882 898 898
+4407342408967

ISBN: 978-93-6783-426-8

Cover design: Daksh
Typesetting: Tanya Raj Upadhyay

First Edition: November 2024

Preface

Quitting Smoking is not just about breaking a habit; it's about reclaiming your life. I didn't always understand this, but life's experiences, both personal and professional, taught me that the way we perceive a challenge determines how we respond to it. Over the years, I have seen friends and colleagues struggle with giving up smoking – some succeeding, others succumbing to it.

This book was born out of my desire to help people see that quitting is not a battle to fight but a shift in perception to be embraced. My journey through self-doubt, midlife transitions, and the masks I wore in pursuit of acceptance has given me insights into how deeply our minds can deceive us – and how liberating it is when we learn to change our perspective.

This book is not just a guide to quitting Smoking. It's an invitation to explore how shifting your thoughts can transform more than just a habit. It is about creating a life where freedom, well-being, and clarity become your new routine.

As you read through these pages, remember that every small step counts and every new habit is an investment in a better future. Let this be the first step towards the empowered and smoke-free version of yourself.

Welcome to the journey.

– Capt. Suraj Tuluri

Table of Contents

Introduction: My Retrigger. My Calling. 1

Chapter 1: My Transformative Years: The Smoking Mindset in the 1990s 8

Chapter 2: Patterns and Triggers 17

Chapter 3: The Power of Self-Deception: "I can quit at any time." 28

Chapter 4: Changing Perceptions, Changing Habits 42

Chapter 5: Emotional Needs: What Truly Fuels the Smoking Cycle 53

Chapter 6: Making the Switch: Replacing old habits with new wellbeing 61

Chapter 7: The Domino Effect – Quitting and Growing 81

Chapter 8: How breaking habits becomes easier with a coach 90

MPower – From Mask to Mastery 100

Introduction:
My Retrigger. My Calling.

My journey as a coach began in 2020, during one of the most challenging periods of my life. I was grappling with emotional lows that felt like they might swallow me whole. The weight of personal struggles and professional pressures became overwhelming, and I found myself caught in a spiral of insecurity and self-doubt. A seemingly small, offhand comment from my boss triggered a wave of emotions I hadn't felt since I was 13 years old - memories of bullying, moments of feeling inadequate, and doubts about my worth. It was as though the walls I had built around those insecurities had come crashing down, leaving me vulnerable.

At first, it felt unbearable. How could something as simple as a comment reopen wounds I thought were long healed? I wrestled with those emotions, trying to find meaning in the storm. But as painful as that moment was, it became the turning point in my life—a pivotal shift that set me on a new path. It was during this period of reflection that I discovered my passion for coaching. I realized that understanding how life works, how perceptions shape our reality, and helping others navigate their struggles wasn't just a choice but my calling.

Habits That Grow Up With Us

Many men I coach today are wrestling with insecurities they've carried since childhood. These men—often in their middle age, find themselves trapped in behaviours rooted in the need for acceptance, belonging, and identity. Though seemingly innocuous, their habits are related to outdated perceptions formed during difficult moments in their early lives. This realization is what inspired me to write this book. The challenges we face in adulthood—whether it's smoking, procrastination, or the need for external validation—often stem from deeply ingrained beliefs we carry from childhood. And the good news? These beliefs and the behaviours they create can be changed.

When I reflect on my teenage years, I remember how many of my friends turned to Smoking as a way to belong. To them, that first cigarette was more than just an act—it was a way to prove their worth, to be accepted by the group, and to feel powerful. Smoking wasn't just a habit; it was a statement of identity. I can still picture those moments vividly—watching my friends light up their cigarettes, laughing, bonding, and basking in the fleeting sense of belonging that came with it. For them, that cigarette was a gateway into a social circle that promised validation.

But for me, smoking never held that appeal. For once, my stubbornness helped me not to compromise my values for the sake of fitting in. I was lucky to have the emotional foundation my parents had instilled in me—the confidence to say no, even when peer pressure was intense. I remember telling my friends that I didn't need to smoke to prove anything, and I meant it. I was ready to walk away from the group if they had insisted. Thankfully, they respected my choice, but that didn't shield me from the effects of their habit. Every day, I inhaled second-hand smoke. And even though I never held a cigarette in my hand, I felt the passive impact of their choices—just as millions of others do today.

One of the reasons Smoking remains so pervasive is because the damage it causes is not immediately visible. The harm is happening on the inside, slowly but surely. Imagine if every cigarette left a visible scar on your face or body—if each puff resulted in a physical wound. Would people still smoke so readily? Probably not. The reality is that because the damage is internal, it's easier to ignore or rationalize. But the truth is, Smoking is silently wreaking havoc on the body, and by the time the effects become apparent, it's often too late.

Our bodies are a gift—something we get for free. Yet, we often take them for granted, using them recklessly, not realizing the long-term consequences of our actions. Smoking, for example, slowly deteriorates the lungs, robbing the body of its ability to breathe and function as it should. By the time the damage becomes visible when the lungs are no longer working correctly, it's far worse than the temporary comfort smoking once provided.

This is the reason why it's so important to come to terms with the reality of Smoking. It's not just a harmful habit; it's a slow, insidious process that damages the body over time. And while it may seem like a personal choice, the consequences extend beyond the individual. Smoking affects not only the smoker but also their relationships, their health, and their future. It's a habit that offers fleeting comfort in exchange for long-term suffering.

Perception as the Key to Transformation

Looking back, I'm grateful for the strength I found within myself during those years. But I also understand now that my friends weren't weak or lacking proper guidance—they were seeking acceptance, just as many of us do. For them, that first cigarette was a way to feel included. But over time, the habit became an unconscious routine, far removed from the original reason they started. Years later, many of them couldn't even remember why they began smoking in the first place. What started as a search for belonging had become a mindless habit—a default response to boredom, stress, or emotional triggers.

Over the years, I've worked with countless individuals to help them quit Smoking. I've seen people break free from the habit, not by sheer willpower but by shifting their perceptions. Once they changed the way they viewed Smoking, the habit lost its grip on them. And that's the philosophy that underpins this book: *Change your perception, and you change your habit.*

How we perceive the world shapes our actions, often without realizing it. Many of us operate on autopilot, guided by beliefs formed long ago that may no longer serve us. Smoking, like many other habits, often begins with a particular perception—a need to fit in, relieve stress, or feel powerful. But as the years go by, the reason fades, and the habit remains hidden in the routines of daily life.

A New Way Forward

What if we could pause and honestly examine our perceptions? What if we asked ourselves why we smoke, where it all began, and what we're genuinely gaining from it? Most people never take the time to reflect on these questions. However, we can regain control if we peel back the layers of perception and confront the outdated beliefs that fuel our habits. Every smoker I've worked with who has successfully quit didn't just stop smoking—they changed the way they *saw* smoking. And when the perception changed, the habit lost its hold.

This book isn't just about quitting Smoking—it's about understanding how perception shapes every aspect of our lives. Whether you're struggling with Smoking, overspending, procrastination, or any other habit, the principles we'll explore together can guide you toward transformation. This journey isn't about willpower or forcing yourself to change. It's about uncovering the beliefs that no longer serve you, shifting your perception, and, in turn, reshaping your reality.

Invitation to Begin the Journey

I invite you to embark on this journey of discovery and transformation. In the following chapters, we'll delve into the psychology behind Smoking—uncovering the reasons people start, how the habit takes root, and, most importantly, how to break free from it. Together, we'll examine the subtle power of perception—how we view ourselves and the world influences our behaviours and choices, often without realizing it.

This book is structured as a step-by-step guide to quitting Smoking and reshaping your perception of habits in general. The journey begins by identifying the emotional and psychological triggers that lead people to smoke in the first place. You'll read personal stories—like Sunil's, Meena's, and Amit's—that reveal how deeply these habits can become intertwined with our identities and everyday routines.

From there, we'll explore **perception as projection**—the way our beliefs shape our actions and influence how others respond to us. In this chapter, we'll look at how smokers often project confidence or relaxation by Smoking in social settings, even though the habit might be taking a mental and physical toll beneath the surface.

Next, we'll move into **how to shift perception**—the critical step in changing any habit. We'll discuss practical strategies to reframe your relationship with Smoking. What if, instead of viewing Smoking as a stress reliever, you could see it for what it truly is: a temporary escape with long-term costs? You'll learn tools to help you identify the outdated beliefs that fuel your habit and replace them with healthier perspectives.

In the chapter on **renewed habits**, we'll explore how to fill the void left by Smoking. Quitting isn't just about stopping a behaviour but replacing it with something meaningful. These practices could be anything from mindfulness practices and physical activities to new hobbies or creative pursuits. You'll read about Sunil's transformation, where walking became running, and eventually marathons, or Meena's story, where gardening blossomed into a thriving organic farm. These stories will show you how change is not only possible—it can lead to unexpected, fulfilling paths.

We'll also cover **the long-term benefits of quitting**—the emotional, financial, and physical rewards of leaving cigarettes behind. Beyond the immediate health improvements, you'll discover the freedom and clarity from breaking free of a habit that no longer serves you. Amit's story illustrates this beautifully—how quitting Smoking gave him the clarity and financial freedom to expand his business and achieve new heights of success.

Lastly, this journey would only be complete with **practical exercises and strategies** to keep you on track. The exercises are designed to help you manage cravings, stay motivated, and build a new identity—one that aligns with the life you truly want. You'll have tools to navigate moments of weakness, celebrate milestones, and stay focused on the bigger picture.

By the end of this journey, I hope you'll quit Smoking and gain a deeper understanding of yourself and your habits. This book is about more than just quitting—it's about unlocking the potential for change in every area of your life. Change is possible, and it begins with a shift in perception. Let's take the first step together toward the life you truly desire.

Chapter 1:
My Transformative Years: The Smoking Mindset in the 1990s

The 1990s were a unique period, especially for college students in India, marking the last decade before technology swept through our lives and transformed them forever. The world was simpler yet more complicated in some ways. For young adults, entertainment was limited, yet incredibly meaningful. No mobile phones were pinging with constant messages, no social media keeping us perpetually connected, and the internet was still a distant whisper, just starting to find its way into a handful of homes. Even television, one of the few forms of electronic entertainment, offered only a limited number of channels through Dish TV. In this setting, life unfolded at a pace where friendships were forged over endless conversations, shared experiences, and indulgences that brought people together—like movies and, for some, Smoking.

College life in the 90s carried a profound sense of newfound freedom. The rigid structure of school days dissolved, and for the first time, many students tasted the liberty to shape their time. Without smartphones to distract or document every moment, students spent their days attending classes, and their evenings and weekends were devoted to face-to-face socializing. Cafés and canteens became communal spaces, buzzing with conversations about everything under the sun. But if there was one topic that never failed to make its way into every conversation, it was movies. Movies weren't just an escape from the monotony of lectures—they were events that shaped the culture, influenced fashion, and provided an endless source of fascination and discussion.

Cinema stars of the time were larger-than-life figures, idols who captured the imaginations of young minds. These heroes weren't just characters on a screen; they were symbols of what many aspired to be—confident, rebellious, strong, and effortlessly cool. And often, this sense of coolness came wrapped in the form of a cigarette. The image of a hero lighting up, inhaling deeply, and exhaling smoke was iconic. Smoking was not just an action; it was a statement. It was an unspoken language of defiance, maturity, and, sometimes, quiet sophistication.

For many college students, their first encounter with cigarettes wasn't about curiosity or peer pressure but about imitating these cinematic heroes. Smoking wasn't about addiction; it was about belonging, about being part of a culture that celebrated nonchalance and rebelliousness. Passing Cigarettes in groups was like tokens of solidarity, more about bonding than nicotine. In those moments, a cigarette became more than a prop—it became a symbol of friendship, an act that brought people together, solidified relationships, and made them feel, in a way, invincible.

The College Expericnce in the 90s: More Than Just Smoke

College in the 90s was more than just an academic journey; it was a rite of passage into adulthood, a time of exploration where boundaries were tested and identities were forged. Without the constant barrage of notifications and digital content that students today experience, the college social experience was vastly different. Conversations weren't superficial or punctuated by glances at a phone screen; they were deep, personal, and involved. The time they stretched out in ways that allowed friendships to deepen over long chats in the hostel rooms, on street corners, or in dimly lit cafés.

Movies played a massive role in shaping the collective consciousness of youth. These weren't just films—they were cultural phenomena that fueled conversations for days, sometimes weeks. In an age where access to films was limited to theatres and the occasional VHS rental, going to the cinema was an event. College students would plan their weekends around movie releases, forming groups to catch the latest blockbusters. The heroes on the silver screen became aspirational figures, their every move emulated by an entire generation.

Smokers weren't simply lighting cigarettes. They were mimicking the intensity and drama of their favourite stars. It was a quiet rebellion, a way to say, "Rules do not bind me." Even those who didn't smoke would often join the group, soaking in the camaraderie of those moments. Lighting a cigarette, sharing a drag, and passing it around was an act of friendship that transcended words. It was about being seen, about finding your place in a larger narrative. The symbolism of that act was far more powerful than the cigarette itself.

But there was another side to Smoking, a darker undercurrent. What started as a harmless indulgence often became something more deceptive—a crutch, a habit, and, for some, a full-blown addiction. The pressures of academic life, coupled with the emotional turbulence of being young, made smoking an easy escape for many students. Smoking provided a brief respite, a momentary sense of calm in moments of stress—whether it was the burden of exams, the pain of a breakup, or the uncertainty of the future.

The Emotional Connection: Finding Comfort in the Smoke

For many students, Smoking became intertwined with emotions. It wasn't just about the nicotine rush or the image of looking cool; it was about the ritual of it all. The simple act of lighting a cigarette became a way to mark the end of a stressful day, punctuate moments of tension, or even carve out a small bubble of peace in the chaos of college life. The connection was emotional, almost meditative for some. The first inhale, the glow of the cigarette tip, the swirl of smoke—it all provided a sense of calm, a temporary reprieve from the pressures of life.

The chemical side of Smoking also can't be ignored. Nicotine, as it turns out, is a powerful ally in the battle against stress, albeit a dangerous one. When it enters the bloodstream, it triggers the release of dopamine—a neurotransmitter linked to pleasure and reward. This fleeting rush of dopamine brought a temporary sense of well-being that masked the stress and anxiety that many students were grappling with. Over time, this emotional and chemical bond grew stronger, turning what was once an occasional indulgence into a necessity.

For some, like my friend Raj, this emotional connection to Smoking became more than just a coping mechanism—it became a lifeline. Raj was the kind of guy who could light up any room he walked into. He was charismatic, funny, and the life of the party. Raj was the first in our group to start smoking. For him, it embodied the rebellious spirit he admired in his favourite movie stars. He wasn't addicted to cigarettes at first; the addiction was to the image it gave him, the sense of power and control.

Raj's Story: A Downward Spiral

Raj's story is a painful reminder of how easily one can lose control. At first, it was just a cigarette here and there—during our late-night movie outings, in between sips of coffee at the college canteen, or after a particularly stressful day of lectures. It was all very casual, something he could stop anytime. Or so he thought.

But as the months went by, Raj's Smoking became more frequent. By the time we graduated, he was smoking a pack a day. It was no longer about looking cool or fitting in—it had become a part of his routine. A cigarette in the morning with his tea, one after lunch, another before heading into class—a rhythm he fell into almost unconsciously. The fundamental shift came when he began needing it to manage his stress. Whenever life threw academic or personal challenges, Raj turned to Smoking. It became his constant companion, his escape from the pressures of life.

As the years went on, the toll on his body became evident. His once energetic and youthful persona became clouded by coughing and fatigue. He began to notice shortness of breath, but like many smokers, he shrugged it off. It wasn't until he was diagnosed with severe lung damage that the gravity of his addiction hit him. The doctors told him that 70% of his lung capacity was damaged, and if he didn't quit immediately, the damage would be irreversible. For Raj, it was a harsh wake-up call. What started as a social activity had spiralled into something far more dangerous.

It was heartbreaking to see someone so full of life come to terms with the consequences of a habit that had taken over his life. He managed to quit eventually, but the damage had already happened. Raj still lives with the consequences of his Smoking, a permanent reminder of how a simple indulgence can spiral out of control.

The First Encounter: Childhood Memories of Smoking

For me, my exposure to Smoking came much before I started college. My first encounter with it was much earlier when I was just a child. It was the early 80s, a time even more devoid of technology than the 90s. We didn't have a television, and mobile phones were still a far-off dream. Our entertainment came from playing outside, reading books, or gathering with family in the evenings. These gatherings were lively, filled with the sound of adults chatting and playing cards late into the night.

I was the youngest in a large family, with cousins older than me. Like most teenagers, they were curious about everything the adults did but kept hidden among them. My uncle was a smoker, but he always did so in secret, away from the family's disapproving eyes. Of course, his habit didn't escape the attention of my cousins, who, like many teens, were fascinated by anything forbidden.

One evening, while the adults were busy with their card games, my cousins wanted to try Smoking. They managed to sneak a cigarette from my uncle's stash and headed to the terrace. I was too young to fully understand what was happening; I was assigned the crucial duty of guarding the staircase, determined to ensure no one stumbled upon them. The weight of responsibility settled on me as I stood to watch, fully aware that their secret was in my hands. From my post, I watched as they nervously lit the cigarette, taking turns to mimic what they had seen my uncle do. Each cousin took a hesitant drag, coughing and laughing at their failed attempts to blow smoke rings.

That night, it made a lasting impression on me. I didn't understand the allure of Smoking, but I could see the excitement it brought to my cousins.—the thrill of doing something forbidden carried an air of mystery and rebellion. It was my first glimpse into the mindset that drives people to pick up a cigarette, not because they need it, but because it represents something more significant—curiosity, defiance, and a desire to push boundaries. While I didn't grasp this deeper meaning at the time, my fear of doing something prohibited stopped me from trying my first drag that night. Later, my stubbornness and family values kept the habit at bay.

The Road to Addiction

The stories of Raj, my cousins, and countless others are not unique. They reflect the experiences of many who, in their youth, are drawn to Smoking for reasons that are often emotional or psychological. Whether it's the desire to fit in, the thrill of rebellion, or the need to cope with stress, the reasons for Smoking are deeply personal. But as these stories show, the consequences can be devastating.

Smoking often starts as a choice—a decision made in the company of friends, in moments of curiosity or social pressure. But over time, it can become a crutch, a habit that is incredibly difficult to break. The emotional connection to Smoking, reinforced by the addictive nature of nicotine, creates a bond that feels unbreakable.

Addiction is like walking into quicksand. At first, it feels soft and comforting even, especially after a long, tiring walk. It may seem harmless, but you're in danger of sinking when you step into it. In the beginning, you can pull yourself out with relative ease. This is the initial stage of addiction, where, with sufficient awareness and willpower, one can walk away before the habit becomes established.

If you wait too long, however, you'll find yourself in the second stage, sinking deeper, and it becomes harder to escape on your own. In this stage, you'll need help—a friend, a support group, or even this book—to pull you out. The deeper you go, the harder it is to break free, but with help, it's still possible.

The third stage, however, is the most dangerous. At this stage, you are completely engulfed in the quicksand, and even with assistance, it might be too late for you to break free. The addiction has taken full control, and the only outcome is complete surrender—an outcome that often ends in the worst way possible. Don't let yourself get to this point. Addiction is not something to take lightly. It is a gradual process that pulls you in deeper, but with awareness and support, it can be stopped before reaching the point of no return.

For those already struggling with Smoking, it's important to remember that it's always possible to seek help or make changes. Quitting can become more manageable when we shift our perspective to focus on the positive reasons to change and reflect on why it all began. Often, Smoking starts innocently, without a complete understanding of the long-term effects. By understanding the emotional reason that led us to start, we can recognize whether it's truly serving us or, instead, taking over our lives. What begins as a simple habit can have lasting consequences, and with awareness, we can start to free ourselves from its hold.

Chapter 2:
Patterns and Triggers

Our lives are like intricate webs woven from our past experiences, emotions, and reactions to the world. Whether we realize it or not, we all develop behaviour patterns early in life, which often shape how we respond to certain situations. People, events, or emotions usually trigger behaviour patterns, leading us to repeat the same actions. Understanding these triggers and patterns is crucial because they help us comprehend why we develop certain habits and how to change them if they are harmful.

Understanding Patterns

Please stop reading ahead and do this exercise to grasp the concept of patterns.

Think about the happiest moment in your life over the past ten years. Perhaps it was when you received recognition at work, reached a personal goal, or shared a special moment with friends or family.

Proceed reading the next para only after you write it down.

Now, rewind to a happy memory from your childhood, maybe around six or seven years old. Again, please write it down.

Now, compare the two. Chances are you will see the same pattern.

If your happy moment as an adult was receiving recognition for accomplishing a goal, your happy moment as a child could be as simple as receiving praise from a teacher, winning a game, or feeling loved by your family.

If you reflect on these two moments, you might notice that the happiness you felt in both cases was sparked by similar experiences—being recognized, achieving something, or feeling a sense of belonging. This fact shows how the emotions and patterns established in childhood tend to carry forward into adulthood. Just as happiness can follow a pattern, so too can negative feelings, stress, and harmful behaviours like smoking.

As mentioned before, my first experience with smoking was when I was ten years old at a family gathering. My cousins had stolen one of my uncle's cigarettes and were daring each other to try it. I remember feeling a rush of excitement—not because of the cigarette itself, but because I was part of the group, included in the fun. My cousin, Sunil, took a puff and immediately felt a rush of excitement. For him, it was different—he loved the thrill, the rebellion. That moment marked the beginning of his smoking habit, a pattern that would follow him into adulthood. For me, the attraction wasn't the cigarette but rather the sense of belonging to the group. In contrast, for Sunil, the cigarette served as a source of both adrenaline and comfort. We both continued to seek out rebellion and a feeling of belonging, driven by the high we experienced during our first encounter with smoking.

Sunil's story is a tragic example of how seemingly small decisions can snowball into life-altering consequences. Growing up, Sunil was always the life of the party, the cousin everyone gravitated toward during family gatherings. His energy was contagious, and his rebellious streak made him seem fearless to the rest of us. As kids, we looked up to him. However, that sense of thrill and rebellion, which started with something as small as sneaking a cigarette, eventually grew into something far more destructive.

By the time Sunil entered college, smoking had already become a part of his daily routine. What began to feel cool and fit in with friends had now turned into a full-fledged addiction. At first, it seemed harmless enough—just a few cigarettes daily, often during breaks between classes or social gatherings. But as time went on, Sunil's dependence on nicotine grew stronger. He started needing more cigarettes to get the same feeling of satisfaction, and soon, it was no longer a social habit but a personal one. He would smoke first thing in the morning, before even brushing his teeth, and the last thing before going to bed.

The turning point came when Sunil realized he was spending more money on cigarettes than he could afford. At first, it was small things—using extra cash from his part-time job to buy a pack or two. But soon, even that wasn't enough. Sunil began to borrow money from friends, making excuses about needing it for books or college expenses. He even went as far as to steal small amounts from his family members when they weren't looking, swiping a few bills here and there from his parents' wallets or his siblings' savings jars. At first, no one noticed because the amounts were small, but it quickly escalated. His behaviour became erratic, and he was constantly on edge, snapping at anyone who questioned his sudden financial troubles.

His health also began to show signs of strain, but Sunil shrugged it off in his early twenties. He would frequently cough, wheeze, and feel short of breath, but he convinced himself it was just a minor issue—and the health issues could be fixed by quitting smoking later in life. "I'll quit when I'm older," he would say as if he had all the time in the world.

The situation worsened after college when Sunil began his first full-time job at a well-established company. At first, things were fine. He was good at his work, and his supervisors were impressed with his skills and dedication. But the problem came with his increasing need to take smoking breaks. Every hour or so, he would disappear outside to smoke. What started as a five-minute break would often turn into ten or fifteen minutes, and his absence started to be noticed by his managers and colleagues. They began warning him that his constant breaks were affecting his productivity, and some of his co-workers even complained that they had to pick up the slack when he was gone.

As the pressure mounted, Sunil's frustration grew. He couldn't understand why people were making such a big deal about his smoking breaks. To him, it was just a way to relieve stress and clear his head, but to his managers, it was becoming a severe problem. When his boss called him into a meeting to discuss the issue, Sunil lashed out, accusing them of being unfair and not understanding his need for a break. His anger got the best of him, and he stormed out of the meeting, throwing his job on the line.

That was the first job Sunil lost because of smoking. He had been working at a prestigious company with the potential to climb the ladder and secure a lucrative future, but he chose cigarettes over his career. After that, Sunil bounced from job to job, never staying in any position for long because of the same issue. He would either quit the job or be fired from the job when his smoking habit interfered with his responsibilities. One of the jobs he lost even offered an impressive salary, but Sunil found it impossible to stay because the office didn't have an easy-access smoking area. His nicotine addiction had become more substantial than his drive to succeed.

Sunil's personal life also took a hit as his professional life crumbled. His once lively and charming personality became overshadowed by irritability and anger. He would get into frequent arguments with friends and family, especially when they tried to advise him to quit smoking or at least cut back. The more people tried to help, the more defensive and hostile he became. It was as if smoking had taken over his identity, and anyone who questioned it was attacking him personally.

By the time Sunil hit his thirties, his health had significantly deteriorated. He was constantly short of breath and could barely climb a flight of stairs without needing to stop and catch his breath. The coughing fits that used to be occasional had become a daily occurrence, often waking him up at night. His skin had turned a dull, unhealthy colour, and he looked older than his years. Despite these warning signs, Sunil continued to smoke, convinced that he could quit whenever he wanted. But the truth was, the addiction had a stronger grip on him than he realized.

It wasn't until Sunil started experiencing severe chest pain that he finally saw a doctor. By then, it was too late. Years of smoking, he had damaged his lungs beyond repair. He was diagnosed with chronic obstructive pulmonary disease (COPD), a severe condition that would affect his ability to breathe for the rest of his life. The doctor explained that the carbon monoxide and tar from years of cigarette smoking had caused irreparable damage to his lungs, and quitting now, while it would help, couldn't undo the harm already done.

Sunil was devastated. The realization that smoking had cost him not only his career and relationships but also his health hit him hard. He tried to quit, but by this point, his body was so dependent on nicotine that the withdrawal symptoms were unbearable. He was irritable, anxious, and depressed, and even though he knew smoking was killing him, he found it nearly impossible to stop. The addiction had consumed him.

Looking back, Sunil often wondered how different his life would have been if he hadn't taken that first puff of a cigarette as a child. What started as a small, seemingly harmless act of rebellion had spiralled into a full-blown addiction that took over his life. It was too late when he realized the gravity of the situation. Smoking ruined his health, career opportunities, and the relationships that once mattered most to him were strained or broken.

Sunil's story is a heartbreaking reminder of how powerful addictions can be and how easily patterns formed in childhood can shape the course of our lives. What may start as a small choice—like trying a cigarette—can grow into something much bigger, with consequences that affect every aspect of life.

The Power of Triggers: Psychology Behind It

Triggers are cues that set our patterns into motion. They can be external, like places, people, or specific events, or internal, such as stress, sadness, or loneliness. Psychologically, triggers tap into deep-rooted emotions, often formed in childhood, and push us to seek comfort, relief, or pleasure in ways we've learned over time.

In psychology, the relationship between triggers and behaviours is known as *conditioning*, the process of learning associations between our experiences and emotional responses. It starts with an early childhood experience that leads to a negative emotional state and a learned behaviour or pattern for coping. The same emotion activates this behaviour or pattern, even in a completely different scenario.

Let's delve into some common triggers, emotions activated and coping behavioural patterns that follow.

Neglect: A Deeper Void

Whether emotional or physical, neglect leaves a deep mark on a person. When someone feels overlooked or unimportant, they might try to fill that void with something that offers immediate comfort—like smoking. Imagine a child growing up feeling neglected by busy parents who are constantly working. This child may feel invisible and crave attention. As they age, they might seek comfort in things that make them feel noticed or essential, even if only for a moment.

One such story is that of *Nisha*, a girl who grew up in a wealthy household but felt emotionally distant from her parents. Her parents, successful businesspeople, provided her with everything she needed materially but rarely spent time with her. Nisha often felt lonely, especially during the long summer holidays when her parents travelled for work. One summer, when she was 15, her older cousin introduced her to smoking. For Nisha, that first cigarette was not about nicotine—it was about feeling important at that moment, sharing something secretive with someone older. Over time, whenever she felt neglected or unimportant, she reached for a cigarette. Smoking became a pattern triggered by the emotional void her parents' absence created.

Abandonment: Filling the Void

Abandonment, both physical and emotional, creates deep emotional scars. A child abandoned by a parent or emotionally neglected by a caregiver who is physically present but unresponsive may grow up with a fear of being left behind or unloved. Smoking, for some, becomes a way to cope with these feelings of abandonment, offering a brief sense of relief.

Take the story of *Rohit*. When Rohit was just eight years old, his father left the family. This event shook him, leaving him feeling rejected and unwanted. Rohit spent his teenage years feeling lost, constantly questioning his self-worth. At 16, a group of friends introduced him to smoking. For Rohit, smoking was more than just a social activity; it was a way to deal with the constant feeling of abandonment. Each time he felt rejected by friends or in relationships, he would light a cigarette as if the smoke could somehow fill the emptiness his father had left behind. The cigarette became a crutch, a coping mechanism that carried him into adulthood.

Rejection: The Need for Belonging

Rejection, especially during formative years, can profoundly impact a person's self-worth. When someone faces rejection repeatedly, whether from family, peers, or significant others, they might latch onto something that makes them feel accepted or included.

Anjali's story is one many can relate to. Growing up, Anjali was a quiet and shy girl who struggled to fit in with her peers.

Social groups often left her out, and her introverted nature made connecting with others difficult. When she was 16, a group of older girls finally invited her to hang out with them. It was an exciting moment for Anjali, who had always longed for acceptance. During that hangout, they offered her a cigarette. At that moment, smoking wasn't just about trying something new—it was about being accepted, about finally feeling like she belonged. This pattern of seeking inclusion through smoking followed Anjali into adulthood. Whenever she felt rejected or excluded, she would reach for a cigarette, reminding herself of the moment she was finally accepted.

Trauma: The Desire to Escape

Trauma, especially in childhood, can create long-lasting emotional wounds. Whether it's abuse, loss, or witnessing violence, trauma leaves a person feeling unsafe and insecure. Smoking, for some, becomes a way to escape the emotional pain caused by trauma, offering a temporary sense of relief.

Vikram's story illustrates this well. As a young boy, Vikram witnessed a tragic accident that left him deeply traumatized. The memories of the event haunted him for years, causing sleepless nights and constant anxiety. By the time he went to high school, Vikram struggled to cope with his emotions. One evening, his friends offered him a cigarette, and Vikram felt calm for the first time in a long time. Smoking provided him with a brief escape from his anxiety, a way to numb the pain that seemed overwhelming. Over time, smoking became Vikram's go-to method for dealing with his trauma. The habit formed not out of enjoyment but a desperate need to escape his past.

Invalidation: Seeking Approval

In environments where children's thoughts, feelings, or experiences are constantly dismissed, they may grow up needing validation. Smoking, especially when initially validated by peers or authority figures, can become a way to seek approval repeatedly.

Priya, a 14-year-old girl, grew up in a household where her opinions were always disregarded. Her parents often dismissed her emotions as overreactions, telling her she was "too sensitive." At school, Priya was quiet, feeling out of place among her louder classmates. One day, a group of popular girls invited her to join them during lunch. As a way of initiating her into their group, they handed her a cigarette. When Priya smoked that cigarette, one of the girls complimented her on how "cool" she looked. For the first time, Priya felt validated. That simple compliment, though minor, left a lasting impression on her. From then on, whenever Priya felt dismissed or invalidated, she would reach for a cigarette, seeking the same sense of approval she had received from those girls.

Routine Formation: The Habit Loop

Understanding how smoking becomes a habit requires looking at the psychological concept of the *habit loop*, which consists of three parts: **Trigger, Routine, and Reward**. This loop makes breaking habits like smoking difficult, as it becomes ingrained in both the mind and body over time.

1. **Trigger**: Triggers are the cues that set the habit loop in motion. They can be emotions, such as stress, anxiety, loneliness, or external factors like social settings or specific times of the day. For example, a person might feel the urge

to smoke whenever they feel overwhelmed or stressed, as their brain has learned to associate smoking with stress relief.

2. **Routine**: The routine is the action—in this case, smoking. This action becomes automatic over time, with the brain learning to turn to smoking as a response to the trigger.

3. **Reward**: The reward is the benefit the brain perceives from the routine. For smokers, the reward is often the temporary relief from stress, anxiety, or emotional discomfort. This reward reinforces the habit, making the brain crave it more and more each time the trigger appears.

Over time, this habit loop becomes so ingrained that it feels automatic. A smoker might not even realize they are lighting a cigarette when they feel stressed, as the brain has learned to respond to the trigger without conscious thought.

Breaking the Cycle

Breaking the habit loop requires understanding the underlying triggers and finding healthier alternatives to the routine of smoking. For example, if stress is a trigger, finding alternative stress-relief methods such as exercise, deep breathing, or meditation can help replace the smoking routine. Similarly, if loneliness or rejection is the trigger, seeking social support or building new friendships can help reduce the need for smoking as a coping mechanism.

In the coming chapters, we'll explore strategies to dismantle these habit loops. We'll replace smoking with routines that support your health and well-being while addressing the emotional triggers that maintain the smoking habit. Doing so allows you to rewire your brain, creating new, healthier patterns that align with your long-term goals.

Chapter 3:
The Power of Self-Deception: "I can quit at any time."

Every smoker you meet will tell you that they can quit at any time. While you may inwards shake your head and tut, knowing the true reality, the truth is that the power of self-deception is ingrained in all of us and has us locked in a cycle of destructive habits.

Our Masks of Deceit

Humans can align their behaviours with societal expectations, often masking their genuine emotions behind carefully crafted facades. This tendency to conceal what we genuinely feel or struggle with comes from a deep-rooted desire for acceptance and validation. Whether acting as the ideal child, the successful professional, or the optimistic friend, people wear masks to fit the expected roles. Yet behind these masks may be someone grappling with anxiety, exhaustion, or emotional turmoil, hidden from the world to meet the demands of belonging.

Imagine a familiar scene: a couple is locked in a heated argument at home. Their words cut like knives, emotions running high—frustration, resentment, and exhaustion swirl between them, each accusation building on the last. The tension is palpable; their faces are flushed with anger, and the kids, listening quietly from another room, know the emotional storm unfolding. It's not the first time they've heard these fights, and by now, they know the rhythm of it—the rise in voices, the slamming doors, the silence that follows.

Then, suddenly, the doorbell rings.

In an instant, as if by some unspoken command, the couple's expressions soften. The anger in their eyes fades, and their voices, once sharp and cutting, turn smooth and pleasant. They exchange a quick glance—a silent understanding passing between them—and just like that, the fight dissolves as if it never happened. Perfectly rehearsed and genuine smiles appear on their faces, and they open the door to greet their guests warmly.

But the performance doesn't stop with the parents. The children, who had moments earlier listened to the argument with worried looks, now know what to do next. They slip into character without a word, adopting cheerful expressions like actors cued to enter a scene. Even the youngest seems to understand the unspoken family rule: *We don't show our fights to others. We are a happy family in front of guests.* No one needs to explain it; it's just how things are.

In these moments, the entire family participates in emotional choreography—each member playing their part to perfection. The parents chat easily with their guests, exchanging pleasantries as though nothing unpleasant had occurred. The children behave with exemplary politeness, offering snacks and sharing stories with practised ease. The home, moments ago filled with tension, now radiates warmth and hospitality.

Yet, beneath this surface of harmony, the unresolved conflict lingers, tucked away for later. The emotions—Hurt, anger, and frustration remain; they've only been hidden behind masks of pleasantry. Frustration is not gone; they've only been hidden behind masks of pleasantry. What's unsettling is how seamlessly this transformation occurs, as if the fight was never real. The lies they tell others might seem trivial—just a way to keep up appearances—but the real danger lies in the lies they tell themselves.

Each time they engage in this emotional performance, the family reinforces the narrative that appearances matter more than authenticity. The parents tell themselves that the argument wasn't significant, that it can wait, and that what matters most is showing a united front. The children, meanwhile, learn to bury their emotions and follow the family's silent code: conflict must be concealed, and the show must go on.

This ability to switch masks on command—effortless, rehearsed, almost instinctual—might seem harmless. After all, isn't it normal to hide our struggles from the world? But over time, the danger becomes apparent. The more often these emotional masks are worn, the easier it becomes to believe in them, losing touch with what's real. And when the lies told to others turn inward, the line between pretence and truth begins to blur, leaving behind unresolved conflicts and unspoken emotions buried beneath the surface.

Self-Deception and the Illusion of Control

Self-deception begins when we fail to acknowledge how far we've veered from our intended path, pretending everything is still on course. It's like starting with a clear blueprint but ending up with a completely different outcome—and convincing ourselves that it's just as good. Imagine you hire a contractor to build your dream house. You provide detailed plans specifying every material, colour, and layout. However, once the contractor completes the home, you find many changes. Painters have used colours you didn't choose, the kitchen layout looks nothing like your plan, and the materials feel cheaper. When you confront the contractor, he assures you that the changes were necessary, even beneficial. He blends truth with justification to avoid admitting his mistakes because doing so would mean confronting the reality that he failed to meet your expectations. After all, what's done is done—and it's easier for him to rationalise than to take responsibility.

This scenario reflects the way many people, including smokers, navigate their behaviour. No one lights their first cigarette, intending to become addicted. The first puff is often just curiosity, a momentary escape, or a gesture to fit in socially. Smokers begin with the belief that they will remain in control, convincing themselves they can quit anytime. *"It's just for now,"* they tell themselves. But as smoking becomes a habit triggered by stress, boredom, or routine, they slowly drift away from their original intentions.

Arun's Journey: A Case Study in Self-Deception

The story of Arun illustrates this gradual descent into self-deception. Arun was always the brightest student in school—who aced every exam and stood out in every competition. From a young age, he wanted to build an image of himself as someone intelligent, driven, and destined for greatness. He didn't just want to succeed; he wanted to be someone others looked up to, admired, and envied. But success also came with pressure. In high school, the burden of expectations grew heavier. Sleepless nights before exams, relentless competition, and the fear of falling short began to take their toll. One day, Arun accepted a cigarette from a friend, justifying it as a small indulgence—a way to unwind momentarily.

At first, he saw smoking as a temporary release from the stress of his demanding life. *"It's nothing serious,"* Arun thought. *"Just a few cigarettes to take the edge off."* However, as the pressures increased, occasional smoking became a daily habit. He started smoking between study sessions, during lunch breaks, and late at night when anxiety kept him awake. Yet, Arun continued to tell himself that it was under control. *"I'll quit after exams,"* he promised himself. But those exams came and went, and the habit stayed.

Over time, Arun built a narrative to justify his smoking. Instead of acknowledging that his habit was spiralling out of control, he convinced himself that smoking was helping him. *"It sharpens my focus. It gives me energy,"* he told himself. Even when he felt the early warning signs—shortness of breath, lingering coughs—he dismissed them. *"It's nothing. I'm young. I'm healthy,"* he thought. Like the contractor justifying the deviations from the original blueprint, Arun told himself that the changes in his behaviour were for the best.

When friends expressed concern, Arun dismissed them. *"You don't get it. Smoking helps me perform better."* His need to maintain the image of being in control became more substantial than the truth of his addiction. Admitting the problem meant acknowledging that he was no longer the person he wanted to be—the intelligent, disciplined achiever. In Arun's mind, the world was wrong, not him. He framed his smoking habit as a tool, not a crutch. It was easier to believe that smoking made him sharper, more resilient, and more productive than to face the reality that it was slowly dismantling the life he had worked so hard to build.

The Illusion of Control

Like Arun, many smokers tell themselves they can quit whenever they want. The illusion of control is comforting—it provides a sense of security, even as the habit becomes increasingly entrenched. Every time Arun thought about quitting, he postponed it. *"I'll quit next month when things settle down."* But the truth is, things never settled down. Work became more demanding, responsibilities grew heavier, and with each passing day, quitting seemed more complicated. This is the trap of self-deception: it makes it easy to delay action indefinitely.

In Arun's case, self-deception also shielded him from the consequences of his actions. Even when he coughed or felt winded after climbing a flight of stairs, he told himself, *"It's not the smoking—it's just stress."* Like the contractor who avoids admitting mistakes by claiming his changes were for the better, Arun avoided the discomfort of facing the truth by convincing himself that his smoking was not the reason for his health issues.

Over time, Arun's self-deception deepened. He stopped questioning whether smoking was helping or harming him because, by now, the habit had become part of his identity. It was easier to believe that he needed cigarettes to cope with life than to confront the fact that smoking was a problem. This narrative provided a sense of control, even though it was a lie. *"I know what I'm doing. I can quit whenever I choose."* The more Arun repeated these justifications, the more accurate they felt.

The danger of self-deception lies in its ability to blur the line between reality and illusion. When the builder justifies his mistakes to avoid making changes, he is no longer building the house the client wanted—he is building what's easiest for him. Similarly, Arun wasn't living the life he once dreamed of; he was living a version that was easier to maintain. But acknowledging that would have required confronting the discomfort of change, so the lie persisted.

Justifying Harmful Habits Through Self-Deception

To cope with the dissonance between knowing smoking is harmful and continuing the habit, smokers develop layers of justifications. They convince themselves that smoking relieves stress or that it's merely a harmless indulgence. This self-deception creates a false sense of security, allowing the behaviour to go unchecked. The truth, however, is that smoking often exacerbates stress, anxiety, and underlying emotional challenges—it is a symptom of deeper unrest, not a solution.

The story of a man searching for his lost keys under a streetlight illustrates this psychological trap. A police officer approaches, asking, "Where did you lose the keys?" The man points to a distant, dark area and replies, *"Over there."* The officer, puzzled, asks why he is searching under the streetlight if the keys were lost elsewhere. The man shrugs, saying, *"Because the light is better here."* Smokers, like the man in this story, are searching for comfort in the wrong places. Each cigarette offers momentary relief, but the real solution lies elsewhere—in the uncharted emotional darkness they are reluctant to explore.

The Blinders of Denial

Despite graphic warnings on cigarette packs depicting diseased lungs and tumours, many smokers remain unaffected by these images. These warnings aim to deter potential new smokers, especially young people, from starting the habit. However, seasoned smokers often ignore these visuals. Fortified by years of self-deception, their belief system renders them immune to these reminders. Smokers may glance at the warnings and dismiss them, thinking, *"That won't happen to me."* This selective blindness exemplifies the power of denial.

The disconnect between knowledge and behaviour is not ignorance but cognitive dissonance—a state of psychological discomfort arising from holding two conflicting beliefs. Smokers are fully aware of the dangers but continue their habit because acknowledging the risk would demand action—an action they are not ready to take. To ease this discomfort, they engage in mental gymnastics, downplaying the severity of the risks or convincing themselves that they can quit before any actual harm occurs.

Denial acts as a psychological defence mechanism, allowing smokers to shield themselves from the fear and guilt associated with their habit. *"I've been smoking for 20 years, and I'm fine,"* they might say. This denial helps them avoid confronting the painful truth: They are addicted, and quitting will require confronting uncomfortable emotions and making complex changes.

Breaking Free from the Chains of Self-Deception

Understanding the psychology of self-deception is essential for helping smokers break free from their addiction. The interplay between cognitive dissonance and denial creates a powerful barrier to change. To overcome these mental defences, smokers must confront the uncomfortable truths they have been avoiding. This process requires more than just willpower—it demands self-awareness and a willingness to explore the deeper emotions that fuel their behaviour.

For some, the first step is acknowledging that the illusion of control is just that—an illusion. Quitting 'someday' perpetually delays the process unless you take action in the present. For others, it involves recognising that smoking is not a genuine solution to stress but a distraction from unresolved emotional challenges. Tools such as mindfulness practices, counselling, and support groups can help smokers dismantle the false narratives that sustain their habit.

Mark's Story: Another Look at Self-Deception

Mark, a 45-year-old businessman, seemed to have it all—a thriving career, a healthy lifestyle, and a reputation for being level-headed. To outsiders, he was the picture of balance: a man who skillfully managed his personal and professional life. But beneath the polished exterior was a long-time smoker, deeply entangled in the lies he told himself to justify his habit. Mark wasn't ignorant; he was well aware of the risks. He had lost a close friend to lung cancer, a man with whom he had shared countless cigarettes and late-night conversations. That death should have been a wake-up call, but instead, it became a part of Mark's growing web of self-deception.

"I'll Quit Soon, But Not Now"

When friends or family asked why he didn't quit smoking, Mark always had the same answer: *"I'll quit soon, but not now. I have too much going on."* It was a familiar refrain, repeated so often that it no longer felt like a lie—it had become his truth. Mark told himself that quitting wasn't urgent. After all, he ate well, exercised regularly, attended yearly check-ups, and even passed his last medical exam with flying colours. *"I'm in good shape,"* he reassured himself. *"Smoking hasn't slowed me down yet."*

But deep down, Mark knew these justifications were flimsy shields against a growing fear. Whenever he felt a cough linger in his chest or noticed himself getting winded after climbing stairs, the thought crept in: *What if it's already too late?* Yet, instead of confronting that fear, Mark buried it under the same old excuse: *"I'll quit soon, just not today."*

Confronting the Fear: The Power of Rationalisation

Mark's denial extended beyond his words—it coloured how he viewed the world. Every time he saw the gruesome images on cigarette packs—blackened lungs, tumours, and stark warnings—he brushed them off. *"That's just propaganda,"* he would say. *"I've been smoking for 20 years, and I'm fine."* The images, designed to evoke fear, had the opposite effect on Mark. Rather than feeling alarmed, he dismissed them as irrelevant to his life, convinced that those things happened to *others*—not to him.

Mark's rationalisation wasn't just about avoiding fear; it was a way of protecting the version of himself he wanted to believe in—a person who was in control, healthy, and capable of quitting anytime. Admitting that smoking had become a problem would mean confronting the uncomfortable truth that he had lost control over a habit he once believed he could manage. It was easier to lie to himself than to face the reality that quitting would be hard—and perhaps long overdue.

The Weight of What's Already Done

The hardest part for Mark wasn't just admitting he needed to quit—it was coming to terms with the fact that he hadn't quit sooner. He knew, on some level, that every cigarette was a step further from the life he had imagined for himself—a life without addiction. But he had done what he had done, and now all he could do was cope. Like a builder who deviates from a blueprint and justifies every mistake to avoid tearing down the walls, Mark justified his continued smoking by telling himself that he had already damaged his body. *"I've been smoking for so long—what's the point of quitting now?"* This thought haunted him during quiet moments, but he stubbornly pushed it aside: *"It's too late to undo the past."*

Coping with Guilt Through Self-Deception

Mark's self-deception also served as a defence against guilt. He carried the weight of losing his friend to lung cancer, knowing full well that smoking had played a role in that loss. But instead of using that experience as motivation to quit, Mark convinced himself that his friend's death was an exception, not the rule. *"He just had bad luck,"* Mark would tell himself. *"That won't happen to me."* This belief allowed him to smoke without the burden of guilt, permitting him to continue his habit, even though a part of him knew better.

The hardest part about self-deception is how easily it becomes a way of life. Every small lie—*"I'm fine," "I can quit anytime," "It's not a big deal"*—built on the last, creating a narrative that Mark used to shield himself from the truth. But with every puff, the distance between the man he wanted to be and the man he had become grew wider. And the more he tried to ignore that gap, the harder it became to imagine closing it.

The Illusion of Control: A Comforting Lie

Mark's belief that he could quit whenever he wanted gave him a false sense of control. It was a comforting lie that allowed him to put off quitting indefinitely. *"One more cigarette won't hurt,"* he would think. *"I'll stop after this stressful week."* But weeks turned into months, months into years, and the day to quit never came. The only way to truly stop, Mark came to realise, was by changing his perception entirely. Instead of clinging to the idea that he could quit later, he understood he needed to act in the present. If there was a cigarette in his hand, it had to be put out; if there was a half-smoked pack in his pocket, it needed to be tossed away immediately. Each cigarette, or a pack, was no longer something he'd finish "just this once," but a chance to decide, "I'm done." By shifting his perspective to see cigarettes as things to let go of in the moment, he was breaking the cycle. Instead of putting it off until a stressful week was over or until the next pack was empty, he finally found the power to say goodbye each time he held a cigarette.

The truth was that Mark feared what life without cigarettes would look like. Smoking had become his crutch—a way to cope with stress, unwind after work, and even connect with colleagues. Without cigarettes, Mark would have to find new ways to manage his emotions, and that prospect felt overwhelming. It was easier to believe that he could quit later than to face the discomfort of quitting now.

The Way Forward: Confronting the Lie

The turning point for Mark came not in a dramatic moment but in the quiet realisation that the lie he had been telling himself—that he was in control—was unravelling. One morning, after struggling to catch his breath while climbing the stairs to his office, Mark stood still momentarily, panting, feeling his heart race in his chest. He realised that the excuse—*"I'll quit soon"—*was no longer convincing, even to himself. The illusion of control he had clung to was slipping away, leaving behind the uncomfortable truth: If he didn't quit now, he might never quit at all.

Mark's story highlights the emotional complexity of self-deception. It isn't just about avoiding the truth—it's about coping with the shame, guilt, and fear of acknowledging how far we've strayed from our intentions. For Mark, quitting smoking wasn't just about breaking a habit; it was about reclaiming the version of himself he had lost along the way. The builder who deviates from the blueprint can only correct his mistakes if he acknowledges them. In the same way, Mark's path to change began when he stopped justifying his actions and accepted the reality that the only way forward was to confront the lies he had been telling himself.

Looking in the Mirror: Facing the truth.

In this chapter, we explored the power of self-deception and how it enables harmful habits to persist. Through the stories of Arun and Mark, we saw how cognitive dissonance and denial work together to create psychological blinders, keeping individuals trapped in their behaviours. Smokers, like many others facing similar challenges, often use justifications and illusions of control to avoid confronting the reality of their situation.

Breaking free from self-deception requires more than knowledge—it demands courage and self-awareness. In the next chapter, we will delve into strategies for dismantling these mental defences, offering practical tools for overcoming addiction and living more authentically. Whether you are struggling with a habit yourself or supporting a loved one, understanding the dynamics of self-deception is the first step toward meaningful change.

Chapter 4: Changing Perceptions, Changing Habits

Introduction: The Power of Perception

> If we want to change a habit, we must first change the perception that supports it.

Before we can delve into the mechanics of habits and how we can break or form them, it's essential to understand the concept of perception. Perception is more than just how we view the world—it's the lens through which we interpret everything, from our relationships to our daily actions. It plays a fundamental role in forming, sustaining, and eventually breaking habits. If we want to change a habit, we must first change the perception that supports it.

In this chapter, we will explore how perception shapes habits, using smoking as a central example. We will examine how changing our perception of smoking can lead to breaking the habit. We will also dive into scientific data and real-life scenarios to provide a comprehensive understanding of this concept.

What is Perception?

Perception is how we interpret and give meaning to the world. Our beliefs, experiences, emotions, and environment influence it. Every individual has their own unique perception, shaped by years of conditioning and societal norms. The lens through which we see the world is not objective; it is highly subjective and coloured by everything we have been taught and experienced.

For instance, consider the different ways we perceive everyday life events:

- **Sadness at a Funeral**: When someone passes away, people generally perceive the event as tragic. Society has collectively agreed that death is associated with loss and grief. Therefore, when we attend a funeral, we naturally experience those emotions.
- In Mexico, a tribe celebrates death rather than mourning it. When someone passes away, families and friends gather for a lively celebration filled with drinks, food, and dancing. It's a joyful farewell rather than a tragic one, demonstrating how the meaning of life events, even as profound as death, transforms based on our perspective. So, it's not the event itself, but the lens through which we see it that shapes our experience."

But perception goes beyond social events—it extends into every aspect of life, including the habits we form. Smoking, for example, is a habit that can be closely tied to how we perceive stress relief, social acceptance, and personal identity.

The Concept of Perception as Projection

Perception as projection suggests how individuals interpret the external world, shaped by their internal beliefs, biases, and emotional states. This concept, rooted in Carl Jung's psychological theories, emphasizes that we project what we carry inside—our fears, expectations, or experiences—onto the world. These projections act as filters through which we view others, often influencing how we behave and how others respond to us. Neuro-Linguistic Programming (NLP) builds on this by showing how our beliefs and experiences shape perceptions and interactions with the world around us. For example, as we discussed earlier, individuals who smoke may overlook the graphic warnings on cigarette packets, unconsciously filtering them out to reinforce a belief system that minimizes harm. This selective attention is a powerful reminder that our internal world shapes the external one we experience, dictating not only our habits but how others respond to us. By recognizing this projection, we can challenge and reshape perceptions, transforming self-destructive habits into empowered actions.

The Tale of Sham and the Lottery: A Story of Projections

Imagine Sham, a lottery winner who wants to share his fortune with random strangers, believing that spreading joy will make his win more meaningful. He withdraws 10% of his winnings, divides it into ten bundles of cash, and heads to the mall with the intention of giving these bundles to ten people at random. Sham's actions are simple: give away the money as a gesture of kindness, with no hidden motives.

The first person he approaches is a woman who gratefully accepts the bundle. *"You are truly heaven-sent,"* she says, overwhelmed by the unexpected gift. Sham becomes an angel in her eyes, answering her prayers in a moment of financial need. Her internal state shapes her perception of Sham—her gratitude, hope, and recent struggles—which leads her to view his gesture as a blessing.

Later, Sham meets another woman in the mall and offers her the same amount of money with the same explanation: *"This is a gift. I won the lottery and want to share my fortune with others."* But this woman reacts differently. *"How dare you try to buy me? Do you think I'm so cheap that you can silence my dignity with money?"* she snaps, furious. To her, Sham's gesture feels like an insult, an attempt to degrade her, shaped by her past experiences and personal sensitivities. In her mind, he is no angel—a villain using wealth to exert power over others.

When both women return home that evening, their stories to their families reveal how dramatically their perceptions of Sham differ. One tells her husband, *"I met an angel today. He came to answer our prayers."* Meanwhile, the other insists, *"I encountered a devil today—someone who thought he could buy my respect with money."*

Perception, Projection, and Behavioral Conditioning

In both cases, Sham's intentions and actions were identical. The differing responses were not due to Sham's behaviour but rather to the women's distinct internal narratives and past experiences. Each woman projected her inner beliefs—one of hope, the other of mistrust—onto Sham's gesture. Their responses highlight the concept that perception is not merely about what we see but also about what we *believe* we are seeing. The women's personal conditioning and emotional states shaped their experiences, making Sham appear either a saviour or a threat.

Connecting This Concept with Smoking

A similar dynamic applies to habits such as smoking. A smoker may light a cigarette to project relaxation and confidence in social settings, believing that smoking helps them fit in or manage stress. This perception becomes a projection: they behave in ways that reflect their belief that smoking gives them control or acceptance. However, just like Sham's gesture, the reality behind the projection can vary depending on context. While the smoker might feel empowered by the habit at the moment, the long-term consequences—addiction and health issues—are often ignored. The belief that *"this makes me more relaxed"* is a projection that justifies the behaviour, even though smoking exacerbates stress in the long run.

In both Sham's story and the smoker's narrative, perception acts as a filter through which reality is interpreted. Individuals' emotional and psychological states shape these filters, influencing not just how they see the world but also how they act and react within it. Understanding that perception is projection can help individuals become more aware of their mental conditioning and biases, offering a path toward greater self-awareness and more authentic interactions with others.

This framework reveals that self-deception in the form of denial about smoking's harms is not about external reality but about internal belief systems. By becoming conscious of these projections, individuals can shift their behaviours and perceptions toward healthier, more constructive outcomes.

Let's take a closer look at smoking, one of the most widespread and deadly habits. According to the World Health Organization (WHO), smoking kills more than 8 million people globally every year. Approximately seven million of these deaths are due to direct tobacco use, while around 1.2 million are due to non-smokers being exposed to second-hand smoke. These statistics illustrate the grave impact of smoking on both smokers and those around them.

But why do so many people continue to smoke despite the overwhelming evidence of its harmful effects?

It all starts with perception. A child who sees their parent or an admired adult smoking might perceive smoking as something acceptable or even desirable. The child's perception of smoking is shaped by their environment and the behaviours they witness. If they see smoking as a regular part of adult life or to deal with stress, that perception sticks with them as they grow older.

Even when a child becomes an adult and is exposed to anti-smoking campaigns or health warnings, their brain may filter out this information because it conflicts with their long-held perception of smoking. This filtering of information is known as **confirmation bias**—the tendency to seek out or interpret information in a way that confirms one's pre-existing beliefs or perceptions.

Confirmation Bias: A Barrier to Change

Confirmation bias plays a significant role in how perceptions shape habits and how those habits are maintained. People who believe smoking helps relieve stress will focus on moments when a cigarette seems to calm them down while ignoring the long-term adverse effects, like anxiety, financial costs, and the deterioration of health. Smokers may even overlook the explicit warnings on cigarette packaging. Despite cigarette packs in many countries being plastered with graphic images of smoking-related diseases, many smokers ignore these images or minimize their significance because they don't align with their belief that smoking is "worth it" or "not that bad."

This bias is why so many smokers continue their habit even though smoking is the leading preventable cause of death worldwide. The **Centers for Disease Control and Prevention (CDC)** states that in the United States alone, cigarette smoking is responsible for more than 480,000 deaths annually, which amounts to about 1 in 5 deaths.

But what's even more troubling is that smokers often pass on these perceptions to the next generation. When children see adults smoking, they begin to form perceptions about smoking based on those observations, leading to a new cycle of smoking habits.

How Perception Creates Habits

We must understand how perception and habits are interconnected to break a habit. A habit is formed when a behaviour is repeated often enough that it becomes automatic. But the behaviour usually starts because of a perception we have about it.

Let's break down how this process works:

1. **Perception**: People start smoking because they perceive it as cool, stress-relieving, or a way to fit in with their peers.
2. **Behaviour**: They repeat the action of smoking each time they feel stressed, want to socialize, or need to take a break.
3. **Reinforcement**: Each time they smoke, their brain reinforces the connection between the behaviour (smoking) and the perceived reward (stress relief or social acceptance).
4. **Habit Formation**: Eventually, the behaviour becomes automatic. The person lights up a cigarette without

consciously thinking about why they're doing it, as the habit has become deeply ingrained.

In essence, perception lays the foundation for the habit, and the repetition of the behaviour cements it into place.

Changing Perception to Change Habits

If perception is the key to forming habits, it's also the key to breaking them. By changing our perception of smoking, we can break the cycle of habit formation.

Here's how the process works:

1. **Identify the Perception**: What belief is driving the habit? For smokers, it might be the belief that smoking relieves stress or helps them relax. Recognizing this perception is the first step toward changing it.
2. **Challenge the Perception**: Is this belief actually true? Studies show that while nicotine may provide a short-term sense of relief, it actually increases anxiety and stress in the long run. Smoking is not a genuine solution to stress; it's a temporary fix with harmful side effects.
3. **Reframe the Perception**: Instead of seeing smoking as a stress reliever, begin to see it for what it truly is—a destructive habit that harms your health, shortens your lifespan, and negatively impacts those around you. For example, second-hand smoke is a significant cause of illness and death in non-smokers, particularly children. According to the CDC, exposure to second-hand smoke increases the risk of sudden infant death syndrome (SIDS), respiratory infections, and severe asthma attacks in children.

A Personal Reassessment

One powerful way to shift perception is to take a step back and reassess your current situation. For example, if you began smoking to fit in with friends, ask yourself if you still need smoking to feel connected to those around you. Chances are that your life has changed significantly since you first started smoking. You may have a family, a career, or hobbies that provide fulfilment and belonging. By acknowledging these new sources of identity, you can start to see smoking as unnecessary.

Imagine the benefits of quitting. If you stop smoking, you will regain control over your health, increase your energy levels, and extend the time you can spend with loved ones. You'll no longer feel dependent on cigarettes to manage stress, and you'll be free from the harmful effects of smoking on your body and mind.

The Emotional Toll of Second-Hand Smoke: A Parent's Responsibility

Second-hand smoke is more than just an unpleasant smell—it's a silent, dangerous threat that can leave lasting scars on those exposed to it, particularly children. The impact of passive smoking extends beyond temporary irritation; it can lead to severe health conditions, such as asthma, respiratory infections, and even lifelong complications. When parents smoke around their children, they may not realize the emotional and physical harm they are causing, both directly and indirectly. Their example becomes a powerful blueprint for their children, shaping how they perceive smoking and influencing their future behaviour.

A Small Story of Harm and Hope

Consider the story of little Aryan, a bright, cheerful five-year-old boy. Aryan's father, Thakur, was a heavy smoker. Every day after work, Thakur would unwind with several cigarettes at home, thinking nothing of it. He believed that smoking in the same room as his son or wife wouldn't really hurt them. *"They'll get used to it,"* he thought, brushing off his wife's concerns. *"It's not like anyone gets sick from a little second-hand smoke."*

But Aryan's small body couldn't tolerate the toxic fumes as an adult could. One winter morning, Aryan woke up wheezing, struggling to breathe. His parents rushed him to the emergency room, where doctors diagnosed him with asthma—a condition that would now require regular medication and frequent hospital visits. The doctors explained that exposure to cigarette smoke had likely triggered his condition. *"Children's lungs are delicate,"* the doctor said gravely. *"Second-hand smoke is incredibly harmful."*

Thakur was devastated. His little boy, who once ran around the playground with boundless energy, now had to carry an inhaler wherever he went. Every wheezing breath was a painful reminder of the consequences of his habit—a habit he thought was harmless. The guilt weighed heavily on him. He had never imagined that something as routine as smoking could cause his child such suffering.

But Aryan's story doesn't end in despair. Determined to change, Thakur quit smoking, not just for himself but for his family. He realized that his actions carried far-reaching consequences. *"I never want Aryan to grow up thinking that smoking is normal,"* he told his wife. *"If I can break the cycle now, maybe I can save him from following the same path."*

Changing Perception to Change Behavior

The key to quitting lies in changing the way we perceive smoking. Many smokers, like Thakur, see their habit as a personal choice—a harmless indulgence. However, when that perception shifts, and they understand that their behaviour affects not just themselves but their loved ones, it can spark meaningful change. Quitting smoking is not just a personal victory; it's a gift to the people closest to you.

Just as Thakur realized that his habit had the power to shape Aryan's future, every parent who smokes must confront the reality of their influence. Smoking around children isn't just a minor oversight—it's a choice with lifelong consequences. However, with awareness and commitment, parents can choose differently, offering their children clean air and a healthier, smoke-free future.

At its core, the process of breaking any habit starts with changing your perception. When you shift how you view smoking—from a stress reliever or social tool to a dangerous and unnecessary behaviour—you begin the process of breaking free from the habit. It all starts with a change in mindset.

In the next chapter, we will discuss specific strategies for replacing smoking with healthier habits that support

Chapter 5:
Emotional Needs: What Truly Fuels the Smoking Cycle

While working in the corporate world, I had a colleague who regularly stepped away from his desk every 20 to 30 minutes, saying, "Let's go grab a coffee" or "I need a small break." At first, I assumed he just needed a break from the routine stresses of work, a brief escape. But after a while, I noticed a deeper pattern: every time he took one of these "coffee breaks," he would step outside for a smoke. His breaks were about something other than coffee. When I asked him directly, "Why do you smoke every time you take a break?" his answer was simple yet revealing: "I just need to reset. It's not even about the coffee or the smoke; it's about filling the void—something to break the routine and calm me down."

His response got me thinking about habits and why people turn to smoking. It wasn't the smoke itself but the act of "filling" something inside—the lungs, yes, and some emotional or mental space that craved attention. This idea echoed something personal for me, and it took me back to the memory of my late Uncle, whose story is a tragic yet important lesson in understanding the true nature of habits like smoking.

My Uncle's Story: A Battle Against Tobacco

My Uncle was a man of strength—both in body and character. He seemed larger than life to me as a child, always quick with a joke, his voice booming through the house during family gatherings. But what I remember most vividly was his constant use of chewing tobacco. He was rarely without that small tin of tobacco in his pocket, always ready for his next "dip." Growing up in a rural area, this was almost seen as normal, a rite of passage for many men of his generation. Tobacco was ingrained in the culture, but what we did not know was how deeply it would ingrain itself into his life—and eventually, how it would take it from him.

As a child, I found the smell of tobacco familiar, even comforting in a way. It was part of the image of my Uncle that I idolized. He was rugged, knowledgeable, and always had a story to tell. But beneath that exterior, there was a darker side to his habit. I noticed over time that his laughter would often be interrupted by a deep, unsettling cough. It started small, but with each passing year, it became more frequent and more violent. We all brushed it off—"It's just a cold," or "He's just got a bit of a smoker's cough"—but deep down, we all knew something was wrong.

My Uncle used to tell me, "I can quit anytime I want." He said it so often that it almost became a joke in our family. Yet, year after year, he continued to Chew tobacco, unable to break free from its hold. What began as a harmless habit had turned into something far more dangerous.

The Diagnosis: Throat Cancer

By the time my Uncle was diagnosed with throat cancer, it was too late. The cancer had taken root and spread before he even realized something was wrong. His voice, once so strong and vibrant, began to fade, becoming raspy and weak. The man who once filled the room with stories and laughter struggled to speak a few words. It was a slow and painful transformation to watch. His hands, which had once been so full of life, were now frail and trembling as he reached for his water to soothe the dryness in his throat.

My Uncle tried to maintain his sense of humour even during his illness. But the pain in his eyes was undeniable. He had spent decades filling that "void" with tobacco, convincing himself that it was just a harmless habit. But now, the cost of that habit was clear for all to see.

I remember the last conversation I had with him. By this time, he could barely whisper, yet the weight of his words still lingers with me. "Don't do what I did," he said. "I thought I was in control, but I wasn't. The tobacco controlled me."

Those words haunted me. My Uncle spent years believing he could quit whenever he wanted, but he was never in control. The addiction had been driving him all along, and now it was taking away the most precious thing of all—his life.

The Last Days

Watching my Uncle in those final weeks was one of the hardest things I have ever done. The cancer had taken everything from him—his strength, his voice, his ability to connect with the people he loved. By the end, he was a shadow of the man I once knew, struggling for each breath. We were all there by his side, trying to comfort him, but there was nothing we could do to ease his suffering.

In the end, tobacco had taken him from us. I think about all the lost moments, the stories he would have shared, the laughter we'll never hear again. He never got to see his grandchildren grow up. He never got to meet my children.

His absence is felt at every family gathering, and every time I smell tobacco, I think of him. I think of how something so small, so seemingly insignificant, can destroy a life.

My Uncle's story is one of many. Tobacco has stolen countless lives, and the reasons why people turn to it are varied and complex. But one thing is clear: it is not just about nicotine. It is about the void people are trying to fill.

The Void: The Real Cause of Smoking

After my Uncle's passing, I became curious about why people smoke and why they feel this constant need to fill themselves with something, whether it is smoke, tobacco, or even vapour. The act of smoking isn't just about nicotine—it's often tied to emotional and psychological unmet needs that shape when, why, and how someone lights up a cigarette. Many smokers aren't addicted solely to the chemical components but to the rituals, feelings, and escapes smoking provides. Understanding the actual reasons behind smoking is a crucial step toward quitting and replacing smoking with healthier habits. Let's dive deeper into the nuanced motivations behind these triggers.

Breaking the Routine: Smoke as a Mental Reset

For many, smoking becomes a way to punctuate the monotony of daily life, offering a mental pause. My colleague's story is a perfect example. The cigarette itself wasn't what he craved; it was the mental break that smoking facilitated. He would step outside every few hours to "reset" during stressful or tedious workdays. Without realizing it, he had tied this essential need for a pause to a cigarette.

The ritual of stepping away from work—taking a moment for himself—gave him temporary relief. But this habit reinforced the idea that he needed a cigarette to feel calm and centred again. In reality, he needed a mental reset, but he had fused that need with a harmful act. This connection makes smoking challenging to quit—because the break itself feels like a reward, even though it's wrapped in the unhealthy habit of smoking. Replacing smoking with healthier breaks, such as a quick walk or a few minutes of mindful breathing, can provide the exact reset without the harmful effects.

Creating Boundaries: Smoke as a Social Shield

Smoking can also serve as a way for individuals to carve out personal space. Lighting up a cigarette becomes a signal: *"This is my space—do not enter."* It creates an invisible barrier between the smoker and the outside world, a boundary that feels easier to establish than verbalizing the need for privacy. For some, the swirl of cigarette smoke acts as a buffer, allowing them to retreat emotionally while still appearing engaged with their surroundings.

This habit can become deeply ingrained, especially for individuals who struggle to communicate their needs directly. Over time, smoking becomes less about the physical act and more about the emotional safety it provides. However, learning to set boundaries in healthier ways—such as practising assertive communication—can gradually replace the need to light a cigarette to escape social pressures.

Suppressing Anger: Smoke as a Release

For those working in high-pressure environments, where expressing anger or frustration may not be socially acceptable, smoking offers a way to release pent-up emotions. When my colleague felt insulted by his boss, he would step outside and light a cigarette instead of confronting the situation, inhaling deeply and exhaling his frustrations with each puff. Smoking gave him the illusion of release, even though the underlying anger remained unaddressed.

This emotional suppression through smoking is common. Anger, frustration, and stress are powerful emotions that demand an outlet, and without healthy coping mechanisms, smoking becomes a convenient release valve. However, this habit can trap individuals in a cycle—using cigarettes to suppress emotions instead of addressing them. Recognizing the need to express emotions in constructive ways, such as through journaling or speaking with a trusted friend, can gradually replace the reliance on smoking as a form of relief.

Reclaiming Power and Respect: Smoke as a Symbol of Control

Historically, smoking has been associated with status, wealth, and power. From cigars enjoyed in exclusive clubs to the cultural allure of hookahs, smoking has long carried symbolic meaning. For some, lighting a cigarette becomes a way to reclaim a sense of power when they feel disrespected or out of control. In moments of insecurity, smoking provides the illusion of importance—a way to assert dominance, however fleeting.

This connection between smoking and power can make it challenging for individuals to quit. The act of lighting up feels like a small but immediate way to regain control in situations where they feel powerless. To overcome this trigger, finding new ways to assert control is important—

through healthy routines, setting boundaries, or participating in activities that foster genuine confidence and self-respect.

Emotional Substitution: Smoke as Familiar Comfort

On a deeper psychological level, smoking can act as a substitute for emotional comfort. Research suggests that the physical act of smoking—holding the cigarette, inhaling, and exhaling—can mimic the soothing sensations of sucking during infancy.

As babies, we find comfort in suckling our mothers or sucking on a bottle or pacifier, and this instinct remains with us in subtle ways throughout adulthood.

For adults who may not have experienced nurturing environments during childhood, smoking provides a sense of security. Inhaling deeply can feel like grounding oneself in a chaotic world, offering a familiar calm sensation. Breaking free from this emotional substitution involves developing new ways to nurture oneself—through self-care routines, meditation, or activities that promote relaxation and well-being.

Companionship and Loneliness: Smoking as a Social Bridge

Smoking often becomes a social act, offering a sense of connection and camaraderie. For many, the smoking area is more than just a space to indulge in a habit—it's a place to bond, share stories, and feel part of a community. The cigarette serves as a social bridge in these moments, facilitating conversations and connections that might not otherwise happen.

For individuals who struggle with loneliness, smoking provides an excuse to step outside, join a group of smokers, and engage socially. The act of smoking becomes secondary to the sense of belonging it offers. However, this need for connection can be met in different ways. Joining social groups, volunteering, or participating in activities with like-minded individuals can provide meaningful connections without depending on smoking as the common bond.

Chapter 6:
Making the Switch: Replacing old habits with new wellbeing

In the journey to quit smoking, the challenge is not only to recognize the habit's grip but to replace it with new routines that meet the same needs. The starting point therefore is identifying the emotional needs that smoking meets for you. In other words, it's less about the cigarette itself and more about what it represents in your daily life.

For example, ask yourself:

- Does smoking help you relax or take a break from a hectic day?
- Do you reach for a cigarette when you're stressed, frustrated, or nervous?
- Is smoking something you do socially, giving you a way to bond with others?

Understanding the specific emotional needs behind your smoking habit is essential. You may find that smoking serves multiple purposes. Recognizing this complexity is helpful because each need can be met through different, healthier habits.

For example, if stress relief is the primary need, mindfulness and deep breathing can provide that same calm. If smoking feels like a social bridge, finding alternative ways to connect with others will become a key goal. This section lays the groundwork for more targeted routines that fulfill your needs without compromising your health.

Now, we'll explore practical and healthy habits that can fulfill these needs, helping you build a life free from cigarettes. The purpose is to offer you a roadmap to replace smoking's temporary satisfaction with long-term wellness, ultimately setting you up for a smoke-free life.

Replacing Old Habits With New Wellbeing: Physical, mental, emotional practices

Practice 1: Mindfulness and Breathing Techniques

If smoking is your go-to for managing stress, practicing mindfulness and deep breathing can offer the same calm without the health risks. These techniques focus on becoming aware of your body and mind, creating a buffer between you and the craving.

- **4-7-8 Breathing Technique:** Developed by Dr. Andrew Weil, this method involves inhaling for 4 seconds, holding for 7, and exhaling for 8. Each cycle activates the body's natural relaxation response, reducing anxiety and improving focus.

    1. Find a comfortable, quiet space to sit or lie down.
    2. Inhale through your nose for 4 seconds, filling your lungs slowly and deeply.
    3. Hold your breath for 7 seconds, staying present with your body.

4. Exhale fully through your mouth for 8 seconds, releasing any tension you're holding.

- **Body Scan Meditation:** Begin by focusing on each body part, from toes to head, releasing tension with each exhale. This practice increases awareness and reduces cravings by grounding you in the present moment.

- **Mindful Observation:** When a craving arises, pause and observe the feeling without reacting. Label it as "just a thought" rather than a command. Recognize the craving as temporary and let it pass without needing to act on it.

By practicing these techniques regularly, you're not only creating a healthy routine but also building emotional awareness and a calm, resilient response to life's challenges.

Emotional Impact: These exercises help you respond to stress without immediately turning to smoking. Just as stepping outside for a smoke acts as a mental "reset," deep breathing can provide similar relief. Over time, mindfulness can become your trusted ally, reducing cravings and fostering a calm sense of control.

Example Scenario: Imagine replacing your regular smoke breaks with a few minutes of deep breathing. The gradual build-up of these calming practices can fulfill your need for a stress-relief break, becoming a healthy replacement over time.

Transition to Physical Activity: Mindfulness is one way to handle cravings, but physical exercise offers another powerful outlet for releasing energy and managing stress.

Practice 2: Exercise as an Energy Release and Mood Booster

Exercise is a proven stress reliever and mood booster, and it also fulfills the body's need for movement—often mirrored by the repetitive actions of smoking. Physical activity triggers the release of endorphins, which are the body's natural "feel-good" chemicals, creating a lasting sense of accomplishment.

John's Story: Transforming a Habit into a Passion

John had been a smoker for years, relying on each cigarette break as a way to unwind, reset, and handle stress. But as time went on, he began to feel the toll it was taking on his health, and he knew he needed a change. When he first set out to quit smoking, he wasn't entirely sure how he'd replace the habit that had become such an integral part of his day. What started as a simple attempt to break free from smoking slowly evolved into something much greater—a passion for fitness that reshaped his life.

- **Week 1:** In the beginning, John kept it simple. He decided to replace his usual smoking breaks with short walks, spending 15-20 minutes outdoors each time he felt the urge to smoke. Stepping out for fresh air gave him the same sense of pause and reset he used to find in cigarettes. The gentle exercise and rhythm of walking began to ease his mind, providing a much-needed break from work without the smoke.

- **Week 2:** By the second week, John was ready for a bit more. He added some aerobic exercises like jogging and cycling to his routine, dedicating 30 minutes a day, five days a week, to these activities. As he pushed himself a little harder, he felt the boost from endorphins—a sense of well-being and accomplishment that helped curb his cravings even more. The positive effects were becoming noticeable; he was already feeling stronger and more energized, finding satisfaction in his progress.

- **Week 3:** In week three, John decided to push his limits by introducing interval training. He began alternating short bursts of intense activity, like sprinting for 30 seconds, with 90 seconds of active rest, like walking. These sessions were short but intense, packing a powerful punch that helped him stay focused and strong in moments of craving. The thrill of challenging himself in new ways replaced the old urge to smoke, fueling a newfound determination.

- **Week 4:** By the fourth week, John had truly embraced his new lifestyle. He increased the intensity and duration of his workouts, committing to 30-45 minutes of combined cardio, strength training, and flexibility exercises. He even started exploring activities like yoga and Pilates to keep things fresh and interesting. What had started as a strategy to quit smoking had transformed into a passion for fitness, and he began seeing himself in a new light—as an active, health-conscious person.

With each step of his journey, John discovered a deeper strength within himself. Exercise became more than just a way to fill the void left by smoking; it became a foundation for a healthier, more vibrant life. His story is a testament to how replacing old habits with new, life-affirming routines can lead to profound personal transformation.

Emotional Impact: Engaging in regular physical activity shifts your perception of yourself from someone dependent on cigarettes to someone in control of their health. It offers both a mental and physical release, replacing the instant gratification of smoking with a sense of accomplishment that's more fulfilling.

Transition to Affirmations: Physical activity builds a positive self-image, but affirmations help cultivate self-respect and internal empowerment.

Practice 3: Affirmations as a Source of Inner Strength

For many, smoking serves as a tool for confidence and self-assurance. Affirmations help build this self-worth from within, fostering a sense of strength and respect that doesn't rely on external habits.

Technique: Stand in front of a mirror and repeat the following positive affirmations. At first, these words may feel unfamiliar, but as you continue to practice, they become an internalised truth.

Affirmations for Inner Strength and Self-Worth

1. *I am strong and capable.*
2. *I respect and honour myself.*

3. *I am enough, just as I am.*
4. *I trust in my abilities and decisions.*
5. *I am resilient and can overcome any challenge.*
6. *I deserve to feel happy and fulfilled.*
7. *I believe in myself and my unique strengths.*
8. *I have the power to shape my own life.*
9. *I am worthy of love and respect.*

Affirmations for Confidence and Self-Assurance

1. *I radiate confidence and self-belief.*
2. *I stand tall and face my fears bravely.*
3. *I trust my inner wisdom and intuition.*
4. *I am in control of my actions and decisions.*
5. *I am proud of who I am becoming.*
6. *I am free from the need for approval from others.*
7. *I attract positive energy and positive people.*
8. *I am capable of achieving my goals.*

Affirmations for Resilience and Emotional Strength

1. *I am stronger than any obstacle.*
2. *I grow stronger with each challenge I face.*
3. *I am learning and evolving every day.*
4. *I choose to respond with grace and patience.*

5. *I can handle anything life throws at me.*
6. *I am in charge of my emotions and reactions.*
7. *I rise above my fears and limitations.*
8. *I am resilient, resourceful, and adaptable.*

Affirmations for Inner Peace and Stress Management

1. *I am calm and at peace.*
2. *I let go of what I cannot control.*
3. *I breathe in relaxation and exhale stress.*
4. *I choose peace over worry.*
5. *I am present and grounded in this moment.*
6. *I deserve a life filled with ease and joy.*
7. *I release tension and embrace calm.*
8. *I am grateful for the peace within me.*

Affirmations for Self-Love and Acceptance

1. *I love and accept myself completely.*
2. *I am gentle with myself and my journey.*
3. *I am proud of the person I am becoming.*
4. *I am worthy of love, success, and happiness.*
5. *I embrace my uniqueness with confidence.*
6. *I forgive myself for past mistakes and move forward.*
7. *I am patient and kind to myself.*

8. *I am a beautiful person, inside and out.*

Affirmations for Empowerment and Control Over Habits

1. *I am in control of my choices and actions.*
2. *I have the strength to let go of harmful habits.*
3. *I am free from any behavior that does not serve me.*
4. *I deserve a life free from unhealthy dependencies.*
5. *I am empowered to make positive changes.*
6. *I replace negative habits with healthy ones.*
7. *I am determined to live my best life.*
8. *I am creating the life I deserve.*

Applications in Everyday Life: Just as smoking may offer temporary confidence or comfort, affirmations can provide lasting reassurance. Instead of reaching for a cigarette to ease tension or frustration, affirmations can remind you of your inner strength and capability.

Emotional Impact: Over time, affirmations gradually replace the need to seek validation through smoking. They foster a positive self-image and self-respect that can grow just as any habit does, through repetition and intention.

Example Scenario: Each time you crave a cigarette, pause and affirm your strength and resilience, letting these words fill the space once occupied by smoking.

Transition to Social Connections: With a foundation of self-respect, building social connections without cigarettes becomes easier and more rewarding.

Practice 4: Building Community Without Cigarettes

For many, smoking is also a social activity, a way to bond with others. Redefining these social interactions is an important part of quitting, as connection is essential for emotional well-being.

- **Alternative Social Activities:**
    - **Joining a Club:** Whether it's a book club or a hobby group, clubs provide an opportunity to meet people with shared interests, fostering connection without cigarettes.
    - **Group Fitness Classes:** Exercising with others offers support and camaraderie. Consider yoga, cycling, or dance classes where the focus is on shared growth.
    - **Volunteering:** Helping a cause you care about can bring fulfillment and a sense of belonging, creating connections rooted in mutual values.

Example Scenario: Imagine joining a book club where, instead of bonding over a cigarette, you connect over shared stories. You build relationships around personal growth and learning, enriching your life in ways that go far beyond smoking.

Emotional Impact: Redefining your social life shows you that cigarettes aren't the bridge to connection—it's the willingness to share experiences and engage openly. These new social interactions build self-confidence and a sense of belonging that is genuinely fulfilling.

Transition to Journaling: Journaling adds another layer of self-awareness by helping you document emotional triggers and progress.

Practice 5: Journaling as a Tool for Insight and Accountability

Journaling provides a structured way to track triggers and emotions associated with smoking, helping you recognize patterns and create intentional responses.

- **Prompt Examples:**
    - "What emotions arise when I feel a craving?"
    - "What triggered this craving—stress, boredom, or social cues?"
    - "How does my life improve each day I'm smoke-free?"
    - "What small victories can I celebrate today?"

Suresh's Story: Suresh was known by everyone as the go-to person whenever there was a problem. Humble, kind, and always willing to lend a hand, he was the friend who would listen without judgment, the brother who was there at a moment's notice, and the colleague who made time for others no matter how busy he was. People naturally gravitated toward him, knowing he would help them find comfort and solutions. But beneath this warm and giving exterior, Suresh was struggling.

For years, Suresh had been quietly battling his own stress. Work demands weighed heavily on him, and the pressures of a demanding boss added to his burden. He was the type to shoulder these pressures without letting others know the toll they took on him. Early in his twenties, to cope with the constant demands of his job, he picked up smoking. At first, it was an occasional cigarette to take the edge off after a difficult day. But over the years, it became his anchor in times of stress, a habit he relied on daily. While he was always there for others, this habit was his hidden escape.

By the time he reached his thirties, the years of smoking had started to show their effects. Suresh felt tired, his energy levels were dipping, and his health was beginning to decline. He wanted to quit, but the habit was deeply ingrained. Taking walks and practicing breathing exercises helped, but only to a small extent. He knew he needed a clearer understanding of his cravings—when and why they happened—to truly make a change.

That's when Suresh turned to journaling. Every day, he committed to noting down his cravings and experiences with smoking. He wrote about his emotions, what triggered his urge to smoke, and how many cigarettes he had each day. He began asking himself questions like, "What emotions arise when I feel a craving?" or "What triggered this craving—was it stress, boredom, or social pressure?" Through this practice, he discovered a pattern: his cravings peaked after particularly stressful meetings. This realization was an eye-opener for him; for the first time, he could clearly see the connection between his stress and smoking habit.

With this newfound awareness, Suresh began to experiment with healthier responses to these triggers. When he felt the urge to smoke after a meeting, he would instead take a quick walk or do a few minutes of deep breathing to relieve his stress. He replaced his old habit with a new routine of visualization exercises, picturing himself as strong, healthy, and smoke-free.

As days turned into weeks, journaling became a powerful ally in his journey. He celebrated small victories, like days when he smoked fewer cigarettes or managed a stressful situation without reaching for one at all. Slowly but steadily, he began to feel more in control, watching his cravings diminish as he created a healthier lifestyle. By tracking his journey and reflecting on each step, Suresh was able to break free from a habit that had controlled him for so long.

Journaling not only helped Suresh quit smoking, but it also helped him reconnect with himself. For the first time, he wasn't just the person who was there for everyone else—he was finally there for himself, too..

Emotional Impact: Journaling builds accountability, self-awareness, and a sense of progress. It allows you to see your transformation over time, turning each challenge into an opportunity for growth.

Transition to Visualization: Visualization enhances motivation by picturing a smoke-free future, reinforcing positive change.

Practice 6: Visualization as Motivation

Visualization is a mental exercise where you imagine your future as a non-smoker, rehearsing healthy responses to cravings and seeing yourself thriving without cigarettes.

- **How to Practice:** Close your eyes and picture a moment when you would usually smoke—after a stressful meeting or during a social gathering. Instead, visualize yourself choosing a healthy response, like taking a walk or engaging in a mindful breathing exercise.
- **Visualize Benefits:** Picture yourself spending time with loved ones, filled with energy, free from cigarettes. Imagine the financial savings, improved health, and the pride of living smoke-free.

Example Scenario: Imagine yourself with family, active and healthy, enjoying the freedom and confidence that comes from a smoke-free life.

Emotional Impact: Visualization strengthens your resolve to quit by creating a mental picture of success. The more vividly you imagine this future, the more tangible it becomes, keeping you motivated.

In these transformative practices, you've gained a toolkit to break the smoking habit by replacing it with healthier routines that address underlying emotional and social needs. Mindfulness and breathing techniques provide calm and control; physical activity offers an outlet for energy and stress; affirmations help you reclaim self-respect; social alternatives build meaningful connections without cigarettes; journaling gives you insight into your triggers and progress; and visualization inspires you to envision a smoke-free future. Each of these methods serves as a stepping stone, strengthening your ability to navigate cravings, manage stress, and build resilience.

Maintaining Consistency: Transitioning from practices to habits

Now let's look at how to build consistency to ensure these new practices become a habit and a part of your life, cementing the path to a smoke-free future.

The 2% Rule: Small Gains Lead to Big Changes

When embarking on a journey of personal change, it's easy to feel daunted by the commitment to substantial daily efforts, whether it's a new exercise routine, a mindful breathing practice, or meditation. This is where the power of incremental growth shines—a practice that encourages adding just 2% more effort each day. Imagine your progress as a form of "compounded interest." Each day, the slight increase builds upon the previous effort, accumulating in surprising and transformative ways over time.

How It Works in Practice

Let's say today you commit to 10 minutes of meditation. Tomorrow, applying the 2% rule, you'll aim to extend that by just a tiny bit—adding around 12 seconds, making it 10 minutes and 12 seconds. While 12 seconds might seem insignificant, those minor increases accumulate. A week from now, you could be meditating for over 11 minutes, and by the end of the month, you'll see a substantial growth without any overwhelming shifts.

This concept applies not only to meditation but to any activity you wish to enhance: reading, exercising, practicing mindfulness, or even pursuing knowledge. By making these consistent, small increases, you keep progressing, subtly building your endurance, commitment, and ability.

No Zero Days: Staying Consistent, Even on Low-Energy Days

The No Zero Day concept is simple yet powerful: aim to avoid any day where you accomplish nothing toward your goal. There will be days where doing your full routine—whether it's 30 minutes of exercise or an in-depth meditation session—may feel impossible. For these days, the solution is a minimum baseline to ensure that each day has some level of contribution, even if it's a modest effort.

Implementing No Zero Days

If your target is 30 minutes of exercise each day, a No Zero Day plan might set a minimum goal of 5 minutes. On days where motivation or energy is low, simply hitting that 5-minute mark can keep you on track. It could be as simple as a quick brisk walk or a short breathing exercise. Even these mini sessions create a sense of accomplishment, reinforcing a daily commitment without feeling burdensome.

Concept 1: How the 2% Rule and No Zero Days Work Together

These two approaches—2% | 2 Minute incremental growth and No Zero Days—can be seamlessly blended to create a sustainable path toward change. The rule keeps you progressing and expanding your capacity, while No Zero Days ensure that you stay consistent, even when motivation fluctuates. By never skipping a day, and always working toward just a tiny bit more, you build a momentum that doesn't break.

Example in Practice

Imagine you've decided to quit smoking and want to replace this habit with a morning meditation and evening exercise routine. Starting with 10 minutes each, you can increase by 2% daily. Over a month, you'll see an impressive accumulation of time dedicated to self-improvement, and on tougher days, the No Zero Day rule ensures that you still give something. By consistently sticking to these small actions, you reinforce your journey of transformation, never allowing a single day of no progress.

This mindset shift towards regular, manageable growth becomes a powerful alternative to the all-or-nothing mentality. With the 2% rule, you achieve growth, and with No Zero Days, you achieve consistency.

Concept 2: The Psychology of Sustainable Motivation: Balancing Hope and Pleasure

Building lasting motivation requires more than willpower; it involves cultivating both hope and pleasure in each habit you adopt. Motivation becomes sustainable when it's supported by a positive sense of purpose (hope) and an enjoyable experience (pleasure) in the action itself. Understanding these elements can help you choose habits that not only replace smoking but are also fulfilling and lasting.

Consider motivation as a graph with hope on one axis and pleasure on the other. Each quadrant of this graph shows how different levels of hope and pleasure affect our motivation:

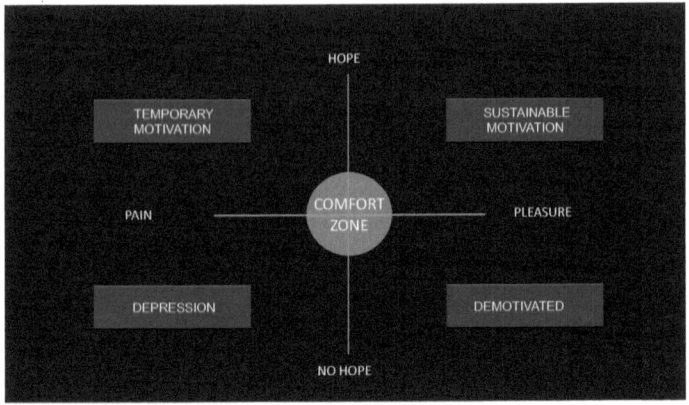

Demotivation (High Pleasure, No Hope): In this quadrant, there may be temporary enjoyment, but with no hope or future purpose, it's easy to lose motivation. For example, a smoker may experience pleasure from smoking in the moment, but without hope for positive change, it becomes difficult to sustain motivation for a smoke-free life.

Depression (Low Pleasure, No Hope): When there's neither hope nor pleasure, motivation drops to its lowest point, often leading to feelings of depression. In the context of quitting smoking, this might happen when the process feels painful, and there's no belief that things will improve. This lack of pleasure and hope creates a cycle of discouragement.

Temporary Motivation (Low Pleasure, High Hope): In this quadrant, people experience hope but not pleasure, often motivating themselves through willpower and a "push-through" mentality. For example, a person might take on a job they don't enjoy but continue because they hope it will lead to a better opportunity. However, this type of motivation is fragile; when the hope fades, motivation dwindles, and it's difficult to continue without falling into the pain of demotivation or depression.

Sustainable Motivation (High Pleasure, High Hope): This is the ideal quadrant for sustaining motivation. Here, the action is both enjoyable and filled with hope for future rewards. In the context of creating new, healthier habits, sustainable motivation comes when the habit itself is pleasurable and when you have a hopeful vision of its benefits. For example, choosing physical activities you enjoy, like walking or yoga, and the hope of improved health, helps create a routine you look forward to rather than dread. Mindfulness practices, such as breathing exercises, can bring a sense of peace and clarity that you appreciate, and they carry the hope of a calmer, smoke-free life.

Applying Hope and Pleasure to New Habits

When selecting habits to replace smoking, focus on activities that fulfill both dimensions. Physical activities, like running or going to the gym, should be enjoyable and provide a clear sense of hope, such as improving your physical health and resilience. Similarly, mindfulness should feel both grounding and pleasurable, with the hopeful outcome of mental clarity and emotional stability.

The goal is to find habits that fit into this high-hope, high-pleasure quadrant. When a habit brings pleasure and aligns with a hopeful future vision, it naturally supports sustainable motivation. This approach transforms each action from a "task to endure" into a positive part of your lifestyle, creating a foundation for lasting change and a smoke-free life. Whatever habit you choose, check that it brings both joy in the present moment and hope for the future—this balance is key to sustaining motivation on your journey.

Moving Forward with Confidence

The journey to quitting smoking may be challenging, but with these tools and a structured plan, you can overcome your addiction and live a healthier, more fulfilling life. Take each day as a step forward, and trust in your ability to succeed.

Chapter 7:
The Domino Effect – Quitting and Growing

At last, here we are—Chapter 7, the final leg of your journey to a smoke-free life. If you've made it this far, congratulations! You've already accomplished something monumental. Deciding to quit smoking isn't just a change in habit; it's a shift in mindset, a transformation in the way you view yourself and your health. Now, we're going to discuss what lies ahead—how to maintain this positive change, deal with the occasional temptation to relapse, and, most importantly, enjoy the incredible benefits of staying smoke-free.

But let me tell you, this chapter isn't just about kicking the habit for good. It's about growth—how quitting smoking is the first domino in a series of changes that will improve your life. So, let's dive deep into what your life can and will look like from here on out.

Long-Term Benefits: The Life You're Building

Now that you've quit smoking, you've set yourself up for a life filled with better health, more time, and deeper relationships. Here's a glimpse of what you can expect in the long run.

1. Health Improvements You Can Feel

From the moment you stop smoking, your body begins to heal. Within just **20 minutes**, your heart rate and blood pressure drop. After **12 hours**, the carbon monoxide levels in your blood return to normal. As the days and weeks pass, your lungs begin to clear out the toxic build-up, and your breathing improves.

Over time, your risk of heart disease and cancer drops significantly. You'll start to notice that climbing stairs doesn't leave you breathless, and physical activities like walking or cycling become much more accessible. You'll have more energy, and your overall health will improve in surprising ways.

2. Stronger, More Genuine Relationships

For many smokers, the habit can create a divide in relationships—whether it's sneaking away for a quick smoke or dealing with complaints about the smell of tobacco. By quitting, you're removing that barrier. You'll no longer have to hide your habit or feel guilty about smoking around your loved ones.

Your family and friends will appreciate the change, and you'll notice a deepening of your connections. There's something incredibly freeing about being your most honest, healthy self around the people you care about.

3. Financial Gains You'll Love

Smoking isn't just costing you your health—it's also costing you money. Suppose you spend ₹200 on a pack of cigarettes daily. That's around ₹6,000 a month, and in a year, you're burning through a whopping ₹72,000. Over 10 years, that's ₹7,20,000!

Imagine what you could do with that money. A family vacation to Goa, saving for your children's education, or even investing in a business—quitting smoking opens up a world of possibilities.

4. Years of your life got back

First, let's talk about the *actual* cost of smoking—time. We know cigarettes are harmful to your health. You've heard that story a thousand times, but have you thought about the minutes, hours, and days you're losing to every puff? Consider this: every cigarette you smoke cuts approximately **two minutes** off your life. Doesn't sound like much? Let's do the math, and you'll see how eye-opening those two minutes can be.

- If you smoke **20 cigarettes** a day (a pack), you're losing **40 minutes** of your life daily.
- That's around **20 hours** a month, or almost an entire day.
- Over a year, those 40 minutes daily add up to about **ten full days**—10 days you'll never get back.
- Now, imagine you've smoked for 20 years. That's **200 days**—over six months of your life, just gone.

It's easy to brush off these numbers when they're abstract, but think of it this way: Picture yourself at age 65, retired, and excited about the arrival of your first grandchild. Your son or daughter is just a month away from giving you the gift of seeing a new generation come into your life. But suddenly, your health falters. You've spent decades puffing away, and now, in the moments you've waited for all your life—

moments where you should be playing with your grandchild or sharing stories from your past—you're robbed of that precious time.

In this scenario, those 40 lost minutes each day suddenly seem monumental. They're the difference between being there for your family's milestones and missing out on them forever. Wouldn't you give anything for those minutes back? When you consider the long-term effects in this way, quitting smoking isn't just about saving money or reducing health risks—it's about gaining the time you deserve to spend with the people you love.

5. More Energy to Live Life Fully

Remember how out of breath you used to feel after climbing stairs? That will become a thing of the past. As your lungs heal and your stamina improves, you'll find that physical activities become easier and more enjoyable. Whether playing cricket with your kids, going for a morning walk, or dancing at a family function, you'll have the energy to do it all.

This newfound vitality will allow you to live your life more fully without the limitations smoking places on your body.

6. Increased Productivity and Quality of Life

Quitting smoking boosts productivity and overall quality of life. Without the frequent need for cigarette breaks, one can now focus on tasks and maintain momentum, whether at work, at home, or during personal projects. The absence of nicotine dependency not only removes interruptions but also enhances mental clarity and concentration, allowing one to work more efficiently.

As a result, you improve daily productivity, freeing up time once lost to cravings or recovery from smoking's physical toll. You'll find that everyday tasks feel more manageable, and you can accomplish more in less time, leaving space for the things you genuinely enjoy.

Real-Life Success Stories

Here are some inspiring stories of people who quit smoking and experienced a transformation in all areas of their lives:

Success Story: Satish's Journey to Freedom and Growth

Satish came to my coaching program with several challenges in life, eager to make changes. While he sought guidance in different areas, one specific goal was to quit smoking. Smoking had become his go-to habit for managing stress, mainly when dealing with his boss. According to Satish, his boss displayed a narcissistic and oppressive nature, seemingly set on making his life difficult. Each confrontation with his boss felt like an attack, and each attack drove Satish to find refuge in his cigarettes, a habit he rationalised as a source of comfort amid conflict.

In the past, Satish would find solace in a cigarette break whenever tension flared up at work. The act of smoking allowed him to detach momentarily, giving him a sense of relief before returning to the hostile environment he felt trapped in. In his view, his boss was the sole obstacle to his peace and career advancement. Over the years, Satish convinced himself that his boss intentionally blocked his promotion—a perception that grew stronger with time. Smoking had become more than just a habit; it was a coping mechanism rooted deeply in how he processed stress and conflict.

Through the program, I introduced Satish to a transformative framework, which included techniques to re-evaluate his perceptions and habits. This framework challenged him to question the role smoking played in his life, helping him recognise that while it temporarily soothed him, it was not serving his health, growth, or peace in the long run. With time, Satish started seeing smoking not as a solution but as a hindrance, one that had cost him physically, emotionally, and even relationally. His perception of smoking began to shift from being a 'stress reliever' to being an obstacle he no longer needed.

As he committed to this new perspective, Satish could let go of smoking entirely, an achievement that renewed his energy, restored his health, and positively impacted his relationships. However, Satish's journey didn't stop there. Inspired by his success in quitting smoking, Satish began reflecting on his relationship with his boss, questioning whether his long-held view of the boss as an adversary was accurate.

Satish challenged his perceptions about his boss's behaviour through self-reflection and willingness to look deeper. Rather than seeing every comment or criticism as an attack, he considered that his boss's intentions might be rooted in professionalism rather than hostility. He realised that his boss's feedback, however harsh it seemed at times, was often centred on improving his work and aligning with the company's goals. This new information was a breakthrough for Satish. By seeing his boss's actions through a different lens, he could let go of the resentment he had been carrying for years.

In a surprising turn of events, this boss—once perceived as an enemy—became Satish's strongest advocate. He went on to support Satish for a long-overdue promotion, commending him as an invaluable asset to the company. In his words, the company could not afford to lose Satish. This recommendation, which came after five years of being stalled, was a powerful validation of Satish's growth and the impact of the perceptual shift he had embraced.

Ultimately, Satish's story illustrates that changing perceptions can have far-reaching effects. By letting go of old beliefs and adopting a fresh view, Satish not only quit smoking but also unlocked a newfound resilience in his career and improved relationships in every aspect of his life. His journey serves as a testament to how transformative the framework can be—not just in addressing a specific habit but in reshaping one's life, health, and potential for success.

Meena: A Mother's Love for Change

For Meena, quitting smoking wasn't just a personal decision—it was an act of love for her children. As a mother of two, she always told herself she could quit anytime. But the habit persisted through years of stress, sleepless nights, and the demands of raising a family. One day, she caught her five-year-old daughter imitating her by holding a crayon between her fingers like a cigarette. *"It was like a slap in the face,"* Meena recalls. *"I realised that I was showing them that this was normal."*

Determined to be a better role model, Meena quit smoking the very next day. It wasn't easy—there were moments when she wanted to give in, but she reminded herself that quitting was a gift for her children, a chance to protect their future. To replace her old habit, she immersed herself in a new passion: gardening. She began with a small vegetable patch in her backyard, finding comfort in the quiet moments spent nurturing the soil and watching life bloom from the earth.

That garden eventually grew into a thriving organic farm. Today, Meena not only provides fresh produce for her family but also teaches others about healthy living and sustainable farming. Her children, now teenagers, proudly help run the farm. *"Quitting smoking gave me more than just my health,"* Meena says with a smile. *"It gave me a new purpose—a way to teach my kids and others how to live better."*

Conclusion: The Best is Yet to Come

To sum it all up, remember this: quitting smoking isn't just about breaking a habit—it's about transforming your life. You've taken the first step towards a brighter, healthier, and more fulfilling future. The road ahead is full of possibilities, and you have the tools to stay smoke-free and thrive.

The key lies in recognising that change is possible. We've explored several success stories of individuals who, after years of struggling with addiction, were able to change their habits by addressing the root causes. These stories remind us that no matter how deep into the cycle we may be, there is always a way out. It starts with understanding the trigger, and from there, we can begin to replace the harmful habit with something positive, something that truly fulfils our emotional needs without causing harm to our bodies or minds.

My purpose in writing this book will be fulfilled if it helps even one person quit smoking. I sincerely hope the lessons within these pages resonate with you and inspire you to make positive changes in your own life. Whether it's smoking or any other harmful habit, remember that it's never too late to break free. And if you've found something valuable in these words, I encourage you to share this book with someone who might need it. One person's change can create a ripple effect that inspires others to follow suit.

In closing, thank you for reading this book. My hope is that it has sparked a change in your perspective and given you the tools and motivation to break free from whatever habits may be holding you back. Take care of your body, mind, and spirit, and know it's never too late to start fresh. Thank you, and I wish you all the best on your journey to health, happiness, and freedom.

Chapter 8:
How breaking habits becomes easier with a coach

What is Coaching?

Coaching might sound like a new-age trend, but it's actually one of our oldest forms of guidance. Think of a coach as a trusted companion who steps into our lives to ask the right questions at the right moments. They help us see what we might have missed, gently nudging us toward new perspectives we hadn't considered. Imagine navigating a thick forest alone. It's dark, and the path is unclear. A coach is like a guide who comes along, carrying a light, asking, "Are you sure you're heading in the right direction?" or "Have you considered another path?"

Many people need this kind of support but don't realise it. In our world today, coaches come in many forms. We have sports, business, career, financial, and even coaches specialising in health and habits. Each one brings expertise in their area, and, more importantly, they bring a unique ability to see things differently, spotting solutions that might otherwise remain hidden. Sometimes, life gets complicated, and just as a friend might see something in us that we don't see in ourselves, a coach helps reveal the answers that we're often too close to recognise.

Why Everyone Needs A Coach

Everyone needs a coach, whether you're just starting in life or at the very peak of success. The truth is, even when people reach the top, they don't stay there by chance. They work with coaches to help them keep growing. Imagine a top athlete—a cricket star, for example. He's already winning games, breaking records, and seems unstoppable. But he still has a coach. Why? Because if he stopped working with a coach, his progress would eventually slow down. The coach is there to help him see minor improvements, areas he can sharpen, or weaknesses he needs to overcome before they become problems.

In the same way, people who are in difficult situations or who feel 'stuck' need a coach to guide them forward. Many smokers, for instance, want to quit but can't quite figure out why they're drawn back to it. A coach's role is not to force someone to quit smoking but to help them understand the reasons behind their habit. Maybe there's a hidden reason they haven't noticed or a feeling they're unaware of, like stress or loneliness. A coach will ask the questions that bring these things to light, giving the smoker a new understanding of their habit and the chance to change it.

The Difference Between Coaching and Therapy

Some people wonder, "Isn't a coach just like a therapist?" While they seem similar, they serve different purposes. A coach works on moving a person forward by focusing on the present and future. In contrast, a therapist often focuses on exploring a person's past to understand deeper issues or heal emotional wounds.

Let's go back to our example of the athlete. Suppose this star player wakes one day and says, "I hate cricket. I never want to play again." In that case, the player might need a therapist. The therapist would work with the player to understand why they suddenly feel this way, digging into past experiences to see if an old hurt or trauma is affecting them now. A therapist might ask, "When did you start feeling this way?" or "Did something happen recently that changed how you feel?" The goal of therapy is to heal or resolve issues from the past.

Conversely, a coach works with the player to improve their current performance and outlook by focusing on what they want to achieve rather than simply solving a problem. Coaching is about envisioning your desired future and identifying the steps, resources, and strategies to make it a reality. The coach might ask questions like, "What do you truly want in your life?" or "What resources do you need to reach this goal?" Through this approach, the coach helps the individual explore not only the positive outcomes of achieving their goals but also the potential challenges—what might happen if they don't reach the goal and how they'd handle that. This forward-focused perspective emphasises clarity, growth, and empowerment, motivating individuals to pursue their vision and achieve peak performance.

Unlike therapy, which often centres on understanding and healing the past, coaching is about looking ahead and reaching one's full potential. Coaches encourage, guide, and help individuals stay committed to their highest aspirations, inspiring them to take actionable steps that align with the future they want to create.

Coaching Beyond Habit-Breaking

But coaching isn't just about habits. It can help with much more, like building confidence, overcoming fears, or breaking free from limiting beliefs that hold us back. Sometimes, these beliefs come from past experiences and stay with us like invisible barriers. People often put up walls in their minds without even realising it. For instance, someone might think, "I'm not good enough" or "I'll never be able to do that." A coach helps to dismantle these mental barriers by asking questions that encourage the person to recognise these beliefs as mere thoughts that can be changed.

A good coach brings out the best in a person. They don't tell someone what to do; instead, they help that person find their way by exploring options, challenging their thinking, and helping them discover strengths they may not have seen before. It's like having a guide who lights the path and shows you the parts of yourself you didn't know existed.

Why I Became a Coach

Readers need to understand why I chose coaching as my full-time calling. After fourteen years at sea and fifteen years working with various companies onshore, I finally decided to take this path not just as a profession but as my true purpose. To fully understand my decision, we have to start at the beginning—with the story of a stubborn, challenging child who would one day realise the potential of transforming lives.

As a child, I was known for being exceptionally difficult and stubborn. My mother often tells stories of my stubborn streak, like when a single drop of milk would spill from my glass. Most would brush off such a minor mishap, but I would refuse to drink the milk, crying for hours over what seemed like the smallest of issues. Stubbornness was my nature, but in those days, I didn't understand why I felt the way I did.

As I entered my teenage years, things began to shift. At around eleven or twelve, I faced a new challenge: bullying. Classmates and even kids from the neighbourhood would make comments, often about my appearance, skin colour, or the clothes I wore. Each word and taunt started to chip away at that stubborn kid, creating self-doubt. Instead of standing up for myself, I withdrew. My grades began to drop, and I felt myself sinking into a mindset of defeat, believing I wasn't enough.

Everything came to a breaking point in eleventh grade when I failed to pass. Devastated and desperate, I ran away from home. At that point, I believed I had disappointed my family and didn't belong. Fortunately, I found my way back by some miracle and blessing, though it was not without lasting impact. From then on, I wore a mask—an exterior strong enough to protect the fragile, insecure person I hid underneath. I was determined to prove my worth, no matter what it took.

My determination drove me to rise through the ranks, from cadet to captain. Those years at sea, from my early twenties to mid-thirties, were some of my life's most uplifting and transformative years. I felt proud, respected, and valuable—my hard work had finally paid off, and the world recognised my achievements. Later, I transitioned to the corporate world and worked for various companies, yet a part of me still struggled with the old wounds from my younger days.

Then, in my early forties, I encountered a moment that would bring those insecurities back to the surface. I was forty-two when a small comment from my boss triggered something deep inside me. It was a minor remark, nothing anyone would consider significant. Yet, it echoed the taunts and insecurities I'd faced as a teenager. That one small moment reignited feelings of inadequacy, and for the next three years, I struggled with panic attacks and anxiety.

Finally, in 2020, I found a coach who would change my life. Working with a coach empowered me in ways I hadn't expected—it was transformative. I decided to pursue certification in coaching myself, recognising its incredible potential to help others as it had helped me. Coaching brought me back to a state of purpose and strength, but this time, I wasn't just wearing a mask; I had genuinely healed the insecurities that had plagued me for years.

It's my own life that fuels my passion as a coach. At different stages, I made choices that shaped me, and while they led to success, they were often born from insecurity and the need to prove myself. Coaching is not just a job; it is where I operate at my highest energy. I do it full-time, helping others break free from their limiting beliefs, uncover their potential, and move toward their true purpose.

Are you S.T.U.C.K.?

My story, while personal, reflects a journey that many others unknowingly walk through as well. We wear different masks, adapt to expectations, and sometimes hide from our true selves. A universal path unfolds in this journey—from a carefree childhood to an adolescence marked by insecurity, to an adulthood spent chasing validation, and ultimately, to moments of feeling clouded or lost. Understanding the stages within the S.T.U.C.K. framework is vital, as it helps us see how each phase shapes our actions and responses to pain and fulfilment. Most people live in these stages without awareness, operating on autopilot and using coping mechanisms to numb the discomfort. Recognising where we stand on this journey can be the first step to actual change, allowing us to break free from old habits, like smoking, and begin creating a life of purpose, self-acceptance, and empowerment.

Spirited (Ages 0-10): Carefree Beginnings

In the beginning, life is a blank canvas, filled with endless possibilities and adventure. As children, we live with boundless energy, curiosity, and wonder. We aren't aware of societal expectations or limitations and act purely out of joy. Like many, my early years were full of spirit. I was free, stubborn, and unconcerned with how others viewed me. Spirited age was a time of innocence, where each day unfolded as an adventure. This stage plants the seed of who we truly are before the influences of society start shaping our identities.

Trapped (Ages 11-20): The Beginning of Limitations

As we enter adolescence, the spirited child encounters a harsh reality—society's expectations and judgments. At this stage, subconscious mask-wearing often begins as we try to fit in, gain acceptance, or protect ourselves. For me, this was when I first encountered bullying, harsh comments about my appearance, and judgments that shaped my self-image. I became increasingly insecure, hiding my true self. Many experience this 'trapped' phase universally, influenced by peer pressure,

expectations, and the internal conflict between self-expression and fitting in. For some, this stage also marks the introduction to coping mechanisms, including cigarettes or other substances, as a way to numb or distract from the pain.

Uplifted (Ages 21-30): Success and Achievement

We often feel in control in our twenties, riding high on early successes. We chase personal or professional achievements and feel validated by external recognition. This stage brought me a sense of pride and self-worth; during these years, I rose from cadet to captain, embodying the image of success and respect. But beneath this uplifting phase, dissatisfaction or unfulfilled needs can be hidden, masked by achievements and the pursuit of "what's next." For many, this is the stage where they accumulate 'success' masks, presenting a picture of happiness while unresolved insecurities remain buried.

Clouded (Ages 31+): The Numbing and Coping Stage

Eventually, the uplifting phase shifts as underlying, unresolved issues begin to resurface. Around this time, many of us start feeling a sense of disillusionment or emptiness. At this stage, life feels less fulfilling despite our accumulated achievements. For me, this clouded stage hit at age 42 when a comment from my boss reignited old insecurities, sending me into a spiral of anxiety and panic attacks. It reminded me of the bullying from my teenage years, showing me that I had merely suppressed, not healed, those wounds. During this stage, many people numb themselves, turning to alcohol, gambling, affairs, or even obsessive routines at the gym—anything to cope with the discomfort they can't quite identify. We go through the motions on autopilot, disconnected from our true selves, rarely questioning if there's more to life.

Knowing: Breaking Free from the Cloud

For most, the clouded stage can last indefinitely. But for those willing to dig deeper, a powerful transformation awaits. It's what I call the stage of "Knowing"—the beginning of true self-awareness and acceptance. This shift began in 2020 when I decided to work with a coach. This journey of self-discovery helped me peel away the masks I had accumulated over the years and allowed me to see myself as I truly am. This stage is the doorway to becoming empowered, finding purpose, and embracing life authentically. For those who reach this stage, it's a time to finally shed the need for coping mechanisms and begin making choices aligned with their genuine selves.

Understanding Our Journey and Breaking Free from Habits

Through this framework, we can see how different stages of life shape our responses and coping mechanisms, including habits like smoking. Often, these habits stem from unresolved pain or insecurities developed in our trapped and clouded stages. If a person starts smoking in their teenage years, it may be rooted in the need for acceptance, a way to cope with bullying or a tool to appear stronger and more in control. As life continues, these habits become ingrained as coping mechanisms to handle the emptiness or discontent in the clouded stage. However, reaching the stage of knowing can open the door to healing, allowing individuals to break free from these habits and transform their lives.

MPower – From Mask to Mastery

MPower is my comprehensive coaching program that helps you shed your masks and embrace an authentic life. The program delves into the 'masks' that men commonly wear—masks of strength, perfection, success, joy, and identity—to hide their true selves. By understanding and removing these masks, we can confront our fears and embrace a life of genuine expression and fulfilment. I will guide and support you on a journey of self-discovery, empowering you to change your mindset, take control of your life, and live to your fullest.

Which Masks are you wearing?

Historically, masks have been used in ceremonies and rituals, serving as channels for transformation and concealment. In modern society, however, men wear invisible masks not for ceremonial splendour but to shield their vulnerabilities and protect themselves. These masks, while intangible, have profound effects on our lives, dictating their actions and shaping their identities in ways that often go unnoticed even by the wearers themselves.

One of the most prevalent masks is the **Strong Mask**. This mask is worn by those who feel compelled to represent the role of the provider, the unshakeable pillar of strength for their families and friends. Under the weight of this mask, men hide

their struggles and emotional pain, fearing that any sign of weakness could undermine their role as protectors and providers. The pressure to maintain this facade can lead to significant psychological distress and isolation, as the wearer must often suffer in silence.

Next is the **Perfection Mask.** Individuals striving to be the ideal son, husband, friend, and colleague don this mask. Underneath this mask lies a deep-seated fear of rejection and a relentless drive for approval. Wearers of the Perfection Mask go to great lengths to please others, sacrificing their needs and desires. Pursuing perfection is a challenging task—endlessly exhausting and ultimately unattainable, leading to burnout and dissatisfaction.

The **Success Mask** represents another disguise, one of achievement and accomplishment. It's a mask often associated with material success and societal status. Men who wear this mask buy expensive cars, luxurious homes, and designer clothes to project an image of having 'made it.' Yet, behind this mask, they might wrestle with exhaustion, burnout, or a sense of lack, rigorously hiding these feelings from public view

An often-missed mask is the **Jovial Mask** worn by those who use humour as a shicld. Being the constant 'funny guy' can deflect uncomfortable questions and shield the wearer from facing or expressing genuine emotions. While this mask can make social interactions easier, it often prevents

meaningful connections and emotional depth, leaving the wearer feeling lonely and misunderstood.

Lastly, the **Imposter Mask** is the most profound, as it involves concealing one's true self. This hiding might include hiding one's sexual orientation, true passions, or other personal truths. The consequences of wearing this mask are severe, leading to a dishonest and unfulfilled life. It raises a disconnection from one's own identity, which can spiral into more severe mental health issues. Understanding these masks is the first step towards removing them. Only by acknowledging and confronting these hidden aspects of ourselves can we begin to live a life of authenticity and emotional freedom.

The MPower Advantage

We cannot overstate the urgency of removing these masks; it is both immediate and critical. Much like a vaccine that shields against physical illness, actively engaging in a program designed to uncover and discard these emotional and psychological masks is crucial for preventing the deep-seated issues that inhibit our personal growth. The body often keeps the score and is the final mediator of our internal struggles—the last frontier signalling the need for change. When our physical health starts to echo the strain of our concealed selves, it is a red flag we cannot ignore. The MPower program is not merely an option but an essential intervention for those determined to reclaim their lives and discover their true selves. It's time to notice these signals and embark on a transformative journey towards genuine health and authenticity.

Here's what the program has consistently delivered:

- A marked improvement in physical health and a surge in energy levels
- Clarity about your life's purpose, along with a rejuvenated zeal to achieve your goals
- Developing self-awareness and understanding others better leads to stronger, more fulfilling relationships
- Abundance in every aspect of your life, including financial stability and wealth
- A new drive to share your talents and fulfill your responsibilities to others

MPower Packages: Which one resonates with you?

Mid-Life Awakening

Most men operate on autopilot. They fulfil their duties and responsibilities and provide for their families as per societal expectations day in and day out. Few stop to question whether the lives they are living, both personal and professional, are what they really want.

At some point - typically between 31 and 40 – they realise that their life feels empty and purposeless despite all the accolades and achievements. The mid-life crisis can range from mild turmoil to a complete breakdown. Men cope by turning to alcohol, drugs, sex, gambling, or excessive gym routines, which may offer temporary relief but can lead to a lifetime of discontent if the core issue remains unaddressed. Unfortunately, many men are unaware that the problem goes much deeper, and it is only when the internal turmoil affects their health that they take it seriously.

Mid-Life Awakening is a group workshop that helps middle-aged men avert the mid-life crisis or snap out of it. The program guides them along a journey towards knowing - a deep, reflective process to understand personal feelings and discover one's true identity – so that they can embrace an authentic life.

Burnout to Balance

Burnout is a state of emotional, physical and mental exhaustion caused by excessive and prolonged stress.

In today's day and age, burnout is common among men. Societal expectations to be the primary provider and excel professionally lead to overworking and neglecting personal well-being. The same societal norms also discourage men from voicing their problems and vulnerabilities, which makes them internalise their stress. Pressure from relationships and financial strain can compound the issue further. If not addressed, burnout can lead to diminished work skills, breakdown of relationships, frustration, deteriorating health and a severe lack of energy.

Burnout to Balance is a transformative program that encourages men to re-evaluate their priorities, acknowledge their limits, and take meaningful steps towards a fulfilling and balanced life. It helps them restore Balance between work responsibilities, personal relationships, and self-care. The goal is not to eliminate stress but to manage it effectively so that it does not affect one's physical, mental, and emotional health.

Addicted to Authentic

Unhealthy habits like smoking, drinking, and drug use often start as a form of relief or escape but can quickly take control, leading to cycles of dependence and regret. These habits frequently stem from underlying stress, unresolved emotions, or societal pressures, leaving individuals feeling trapped, disconnected, and often ashamed. Many find themselves unable to break free because these habits have become coping mechanisms ingrained in their daily lives.

Addicted to Authentic is a transformative program designed to empower individuals to identify the root causes behind their habits, understand the impact on their lives, and cultivate the inner strength to make lasting changes and live authentic lives. This program encourages clients to replace harmful habits with healthier, fulfilling alternatives, fostering resilience and purpose. Rather than just focusing on eliminating these habits, it emphasises building self-awareness, managing stress effectively, and creating a lifestyle that supports well-being in every aspect—physical, mental, and emotional.

Through Addicted to Authentic, participants gain the tools to reclaim control over their lives, replace harmful behaviours with healthy ones, and ultimately thrive with renewed self-respect and confidence. This program is not about restriction; it's about freedom and empowering clients to live on their own terms, free from dependency and aligned with their goals and values.

Free Discovery Call

Before we part ways, I'd like to leave you with one final thought: transformation begins with a single step. If anything in these pages has resonated with you, sparked a desire for change, or made you think differently about your life journey, I invite you to reach out. A free discovery call is an opportunity to connect, explore your goals, and discuss how coaching can support you in achieving the balanced, fulfilling life you deserve.

Please feel free to reach out to me using the contact details provided below. I look forward to hearing from you, listening, and helping you move toward the life you envision.

Thank you for reading these pages and opening yourself to new perspectives. Remember, your story is yours to write; each day is a new chance to shape it. Let's begin this journey of growth and self-discovery together.

"The journey of a thousand miles begins with a single step." — Lao Tzu.

Website: www.surajtuluri.com
Email: talktome@surajtuluri.com
Instagram: @tulurism
LinkedIn: www.linkedin.com/in/capt-surajmani-tuluri

www.ingramcontent.com/pod-product-compliance
Lightning Source LLC
LaVergne TN
LVHW041533070526
838199LV00046B/1649